the

house

on

childress

street

A MEMOIR

kenji jasper

harlem moon
broadway books
new york

Published by Harlem Moon, an imprint of Broadway Books, a division of Random House, Inc.

PRINTED IN THE UNITED STATES OF AMERICA

HARLEM MOON, BROADWAY BOOKS, and the HARLEM MOON logo, depicting a moon and a woman, are trademarks of Random House, Inc. The figure in the Harlem Moon logo is inspired by a graphic design by Aaron Douglas (1899–1979).

Visit our website at www.harlemmoon.com

First edition published 2005.

Photographs courtesy of the author.

Book design by Jennifer Ann Daddio

Library of Congress Cataloging-in-Publication Data

Jasper, Kenji.
The house on Childress Street : a memoir / Kenji Jasper.—1st ed.
p. cm.
1. Langley, Jesse James. 2. African Americans—Biography. 3. Grandfathers—United States—Biography. 4. African American families.
5. Southern States—Biography. 6. Washington (D.C.)—Biography. 7. Brooklyn (New York, N.Y.)—Biography. 8. Jasper, Kenji. 9. Jasper, Kenji—Family. 10. Grandchildren—United States—Biography. I. Title.
E185.97.L25J37 2006
973'.0496073'0092—dc22
2005050358

ISBN 0-7679-1679-4

10 9 8 7 6 5 4 3 2 1

for

"big jes"

and the legend of

john hunley—

you just stepped off

a brand-new train

of your own

acknowledgments

In a year of worsts and bests, when downs and ups could not often be discerned and editors and outlines changed like clothes, there are so many I must thank for the energy that has allowed me to be here. First and foremost, all praise to the Creator God my father, to Angela and Melvin for making me, and to Mel Sr., Anne, Sally, and Jesse for making them and sharing their lives with their grandchild. More thanks go to Tony, Junie, Gary, Aunts Jackie and Loretta, Latanya, Jeanette, Karen, Lil' Jay, Bruh, James, Marvin, Curtis, Ashley, Christine, Latoya, and Daphne for giving me the time and for telling their stories. I thank Janet Hill for believing in this idea when other, less open minds aimed to feed it to the wolves. Shoutouts to Wood, Big Rich, Konata, Chanel, Jones, Mill, Kendra, Suzanne, Baba Steve, Iya Sabrina, Coco, Adele,

Mike Gonzalez, Bob Morales, Big Rob J, J-Thrill, Adam Glass, Suheir Hammad, Becky Bennett, and George for helping me. But most of all I thank the Lone Ranger for being patient with me in the nights and mornings that it all had to come apart before reassembling itself in perfect order.

the

house

on

childress

street

intro

It starts out so small: a square of wood-topped table, a white candle, and a glass of water. The table and the area around it are sectioned off with a curved line of cascarilla chalk. Then for good measure you add framed pictures or the written names of all of those in your family who have passed on.

In doing this, if you believe in it, you are creating a bridge between our world and the other, a portal through which we can communicate with our ancestors. I have chosen a photograph of the man I wish to hear me, a picture I took myself as he turned the corner from his kitchen into the dining room on one of my usual Sunday visits.

Now there is movement all around me, the brushing of invisible leaves across my arms and legs. Intuition tells me that he is nervous, that he doesn't want anyone putting his story into words. So I speak to the deceased. I call his name: Jesse James Langley, Sr., my grandfather. The spoken word is more powerful than we will ever know. The invisible leaves center themselves. He is listening.

I tell him that this is not about judging him, that I am not some muckraking journalist looking to ruin his memory. I tell him how much I love him, that the world should know all that he did to make a better life for his family. I tell him all of this knowing that it will not make him any less apprehensive about what I have chosen to do. I do it out of respect. Without him I wouldn't be here. But to start, to give you a clearer idea of who he is, I'll tell you a story.

I was sixteen years old and I needed a car. My senior year of high school was on the way and I was determined to join the ranks of my classmates who wheeled it to their places of adolescent learning. An entire summer of having to beg my mother to lend me her car had placed me on the verge of a nervous breakdown.

I wanted to be able to see that girl across town (if there was ever going to be one) at 9 p.m. on a Tuesday. I wanted to drive to my father's house in P.G. county on the weeks I wasn't staying with him. I wanted emancipation. And I'd been saving that whole summer to secede from Angela Jasper's union.

I was tired of asking, sick of those nauseous moments when the "to be or not to be" was all up to her. I hated answering all the questions. I hated when my still-developing values clashed with the current law of the land. I wanted to escape, turn a key, and head toward the sunset. Set out for adventure and a life of my own. So, armed with a handful of hundreds, I was ready to score the ride of my dreams at the Capital City Car auction, where lemons and junkers were auctioned off every other Saturday of the month at an aircraft hangar–like building.

Both Mom and her brother Junie had told me that my grandfather was the man when it came to cars. Every ride he'd owned had been bought used, fixed up, and driven for a million miles without his ever spending as much as it would've cost to get it new. Thus anything he said in relation to the automotive was law, and I was to abide by his word if I knew what was good for me.

My grandfather watched silently as the cars came in. And I watched him, trusting in his expertise, because all I cared about was that the tape deck worked and that the thing started up when I turned the key.

A periwinkle '88 Chevy Corsica came into view, a near twin to the one my mother owned. It had the all-important tape player and a good set of speakers. The paint wasn't chipped, and the engine hummed like a housewife doing laundry; everything a teenage boy could have wanted for getting him from A to B.

"We're gonna get that car for five hundred," he informed me, those being nine of the maybe thirty words he'd uttered in the day thus far. "But no matter what they start talkin', we ain't goin' past five hundred."

There was a clamoring of voices as the object of my affection stopped right in front of us. Bidding hands rose as the auctioneer announced a starting price of $200. It then rose to $350, and then $410. But I didn't watch the crowd. I didn't even stare at the idling specimen itself. My eyes were on my mother's father, who remained stoic despite the close approach of our target number.

Didn't he know how much was riding on this outing? Summer was ending. Senior year was calling. I was going to kill myself if I had to come out of one more house party and see my father dozing off at the curb with his hazards on. This man had to save the day.

Yet the next thing I knew the bids were at $550, $620, $725, and finally at $800 when some lady the size of two Della Reeses rolled off with *my* car.

I turned to my supposed savior in disbelief, waiting for an apology, an explanation, or anything other than his dead silence. I could've matched the woman's offer. I had enough dough, even if it would've left me in the lurch for tags and registration. But there was no way that I was going to go against him, because no one did, not my mother, not my uncles, and not even his own wife.

Besides, everything else that came up for bid was garbage, and he and I both knew it. So when the last ride came up to the front, a '78 Honda Accord with the worst rust problem I'd ever seen, he motioned me toward his car without a word. It was over.

My mind floated somewhere between anger and disbelief. I was trapped between having respect for my elder and wanting to put him in a sleeper hold. Maybe he'd seen something. Maybe his Mr. Goodwrench spider sense had got wind of some flaw in that Corsica, something invisible to my virgin eyes. If so, I needed to hear him say it. I needed to hear him say anything.

"How much did they sell that car for?" he asked as we headed across New York Ave. toward Mount Olivet Road, the gateway to his home.

"Eight hundred," I said, impatiently awaiting his explanation. He looked straight ahead for a beat, as if he were contemplating his reply. I had exactly eight hundred–dollar bills in my pocket.

"You know, it might have been worth that," he said casually. "It might've been worth goin' up to eight hundred."

I couldn't believe it. Now he was backpedaling. Now he was admitting that he might've made a mistake as if it didn't matter, as if his first grandson wasn't going to suffer severely as a result of his decision to shake the dice.

But to him, it wasn't about me, or the car. It was about his sense of how things should be. If he couldn't get the ride for $500, then he wouldn't get it at all, no matter how much I, his eldest grandson, might be disappointed. He needed to have things his way. My dreams were an inadvertent casualty. It would be another four years before I got my first ride, a shabby '88 Honda CRX with hubcaps the previous owner had spray-painted blue.

I never told him how I felt that day because he didn't seem to be someone who would respond to emotion. I imagine that his reaction to a crying child in his arms would be to hand it to the closest woman, because she would know what to do. Things were what they were, and you just had to deal with them.

The episode came and went. Life went on. My mother told me that this was how my grandfather did things, and that I, like everyone else, had to get used to it. Besides, I might need him again somewhere down the line. Sure enough, I did. More than once.

Anyone who knew Jesse Langley can tell you a story about his resolve, about his reticence, and about how he could always be found on his front porch smoking a square and watching time float away with that stream of smoke headed toward the stratosphere. But they can't tell you how he came to be that way, the hows and whys that made him what he was. Neither could I, at least not yet.

As a boy I stayed away from him as much as possible. I dreaded my obligatory trips to his upstairs abode to say "hello." He seemed so cold and distant, as if he was less of this world than of some other, as if he were biding his time for some greater journey beyond his years spent on this plane. He treated those he loved most with what seemed to be the utmost ambivalence, as if they were both treasure and burden all at once. How could my mother have been his child? How could my grandmother have lived with him for so long?

This was a constant meditation within my developing mind. As I went from boy to man it got more difficult to bear the uncertainty that washed over me whenever he entered a room. Would he be naughty or nice? Would he help or hurt? It often seemed as if he could never be one way without being the other, and for the very short life of me I couldn't understand why.

By the time this is published, I will be thirty years old, close to the age he was when my mother, his first child, was born. I want a wife and a family and a home with my name on the deed. But I also want peace, which is something I don't think he ever had. It's often said that you can't have a future until you know your past. That's a perfect statement to describe the descendants of a people who were stolen from the land and culture that defined them. Thus, it just as easily describes me.

I am searching for a man who is part of myself, a life forever etched into my genetic code like letters chiseled into smooth stone. I am his future, but I do not know his past. And I cannot go forward until I do.

start

"I'm the Lone Ranger," he had said to me on one of the last nights I saw him, Christmas Day 2002. Seated in the cushioned metal chair in his bedroom, he faced himself in a mirror older than he was. His bedroom was not a masterpiece of interior design: a twin bed without sheets, an antique dresser filled with broken watches, a cluttered rack of suits, slacks, and shoes that spilled out onto the carpeted floor.

He wore a bright red V-neck sweater over a striped dress shirt, with a pair of gray double-knit pants. The toes of his suede loafers had been cut away, to give the shoes the comfort of slippers. Needless to say, he was not a fashion plate of any kind. But he was determined to remain where he was, up in that room, despite the fact that his entire family was preparing for Christmas dinner a level below.

"Granddaddy loves you, Ken,"

he would always say, releasing the words into any moment of silence where it might fit. He would say the same to my young cousin, Jesse III, but rarely to any of his own children, at least not in my presence. And I had never *ever* heard him say it to his wife.

I stood in the entrance to his room on that Christmas night, having given him the hug and kiss on the cheek he had always demanded from me since I was a little boy. Back then, the stubble on his cheeks had been a frightening abrasion to one ignorant about the nature of facial hair.

"You doin' alright?" he'd ask me. Then I'd tell him that I was fine. Then he'd give me a dollar bill. After a few years it was a five, and eventually a ten. And then Mom and I would leave for home. But I always knew, for certain, that I would see Granddaddy Jesse again, even if his presence kind of frightened me. His self-enforced isolation from everyone was too strange for a young boy to comprehend.

But I was a grown man when we had our last real talk on that last Christmas. I had finished school. I had written two books and lived in five different cities. There were no more ten-dollar bills, no more requests for help with the $500 I needed for the red hot laptop I wanted to buy, or the trip to Mexico, or the rent money my shaky career as a freelance scribe made me short on every once in a while. That last time we talked about life, and family, and about how those who love a drug addict often suffer more than the addict does himself.

The addict himself was seated a level below, somewhere between sleep and consciousness due to the chemical crawling through his veins. We spoke of another of his sons as well, the one who was watching his chickens home and roosting in the living room, as the mother of his firstborn scowled at his first wife, while he did his best to remain emotionless.

"I can't be in there with that," my grandfather said of the various tensions just below us. "'Cause that ain't right."

Christmas was the one time of year when we all had something to smile about, the one time we all tried to put our differences aside and just be together as a family. Yet more often than not Granddad did not sit among us, choosing instead to dine after we were finished, or to take his meal at the tiny table in the kitchen, alone.

But that night I was determined to have things go down the right way. I wanted to see him and that red sweater of his at the head of the table, with my grandma at the other end, and grace being said, and all of us being together as a family. For some reason it mattered more to me then than it had in my entire little life.

"You need to be down there," I told him, still standing in the doorway. He stared at his reflection in the mirror as if the silvered glass were the gateway to another dimension.

"You're the head of the family," I continued. "We can't do it if you're not down there."

My mother called up to me from the level below. And I promised him that I'd return to continue our convo. But in the midst of aunts and uncles, my cousin Jesse III (known by all as Lil' Jay), and Mom and Grandma, I never made it back up to see him. But when the time came to eat, when all of us were seated at the family table, Jesse James Langley, Sr., was at the head of it, saying grace and asking for a bigger helping of the best stuffing in the world.

My wish, the first of two that evening, had been granted. The second, for him to help me with a book I wanted to write—help that required the two of us to travel to his hometown of Greenville, NC—was not. I saw him one last time two days later, kissed him, hugged him, and told him how much I was looking forward to the trip we'd scheduled for March of '03. Then I was off, back to Brooklyn, and the struggling writer's life that awaited me there. I got the call less than forty-eight hours later.

Fingers to numbered buttons to the satellite up in space that sent a signal back down through the heavens and into my Bed-Stuy living room. The receiving device, however, was in the Off position, and the cords had been removed from the land line. I had promised the lady in my life a night without interruption, a night where she could have me all to herself, away from work, family, and friends, parts of my life with which she always felt the need to compete.

I didn't get the digital envelope until the sun was high in the sky the next morning, while I was on my way to cash a check, the last bit of dough I had in the world. Now that cash was needed for a purpose, to return to the place I'd just come back from less than two days before.

"We're droppin' like flies," the man said to my mother, grandmother, and me. He was in his eighties, if not older, his eyes magnified by thick lenses in frames of a style that had come and gone long before I was born. The man had worked alongside my grandfather at Washington, DC's Embassy Dairy more than forty years earlier. So, like the rest of us, he was there at Community United Methodist Church paying his respects, sending his friend home the right way.

I wasn't going to cry. I didn't even feel the urge as the body of my grandfather lay a few feet before me. I was too focused on my mother's tears, on the blank expression I hadn't expected from the wife of the deceased. I had to be in control. I had to be a man while the people passed to view the body. But the woman I loved then stopped before she got to the casket. The woman I then called mine turned toward me, offering the most compassionate smile I'd ever seen, her understanding absolute in a single action. She put her lips to my hand, and the tears came forth, rescuing me from the most evil of my enemies: pride.

Michelle Clark, a friend of the family, sang a rendition of "I Got a New Home" that reached the heavens, stirring the hundreds of mourners into a cyclone of the Holy Spirit. Scriptures were read, as were letters and cards from those who held the deceased dear. Prayers were said and the eulogy, the minister's warranted excuse for an impromptu sermon, was delivered. And finally, before the pallbearers loaded the body into the cab of the hearse, before the gathered multitudes left the church to become regular people again, the floor was opened for final words. And I stood.

I wasn't nervous, not even with the drying tears on my face. Deep down I thought that what I had to say would somehow make a difference in how the man in the casket would be perceived after this, his final day in church, was over.

I talked about how much he loved his grandchildren, my cousin Jay and me, and Jeanette, the daughter my uncle Gary didn't know he had for almost thirty years. I reminded everyone of the image most had of the man in their minds, of him seated on the porch of his house on Childress Street on afternoons and evenings, smoking a Lucky Strike and looking out over the property that he held the deed to, with the playground, the center of the neighborhood, just across the street. I said that he was a man who expressed his love through work, through providing for his wife and children, but not necessarily by saying the tender words that most human beings in a family need to hear to feel like they belong.

The words weren't as much for myself as they were for those seated around me, for his wife and children, and my father, the former son-in-law sitting in the other pew. My voice was a conduit for what they couldn't articulate, a summary of the thoughts and feelings recounted in the five days leading up to his final farewell. Had it been up to me, a matter of telling my own point of view, I would have barely offered two sentences. Because all I had was a composite sketch of the man, a gray outline with little color for clarity.

I looked out at all the faces, eyes that knew him, each contributing a shiny penny to the bank of his memory. They agreed that he had been a man of few words, that he had been a soul the larger world might have overlooked though his presence had been so crucial in making our worlds complete. Somewhere within those thoughts I came to a very important realization: that I did not know enough about the man without whom I would not be. I did not know enough about the blood that ran through my own veins.

Within an hour the casket was laid atop its proper plot, adorned with colored carnations placed between its handles by the hands of loved ones. Then we turned to walk away from he who days before had been among us, trying to assess the hollow feeling as we headed back to the church for the repast.

"They killin' me with this," my uncle Gary smiled as he took in a mouthful of someone's homemade corn pudding, tiny pieces of the dessert sticking to the corners of his mouth.

With Black folks and food come smiles and words. We took seats at folding tables adorned with plastic cutlery and pitchers of fruit punch. There were collard greens and baked chicken, turkey, green beans, mashed potatoes, and a choice among the many cakes that had been delivered to the family house as an offering for our grief.

The widow sat at the head of us all, dressed in the purest black I'd ever seen.

"So when you gon' get you a new boyfriend, Sally?" my grandmother's niece, Cordelia, inquired. The widow exploded in laughter and the family followed suit.

Whenever she and the Lone Ranger were fighting, my grandmother had always joked about getting a new man. We all laughed so easily because we knew how much of a joke her joke really was. She is and always will be dedicated to the man whose ring she wore for the first time more than sixty years ago.

It didn't feel like he was dead, because we did nothing but remember him when he was alive, continuing his life through our own mouths and words, spreading the energy that was once only his across the family name, further fertilizing its still rich soil.

I've come to learn that grief is protean, ever evolving as it winds through one's heart and head. It creates and destroys all in its path as it moves toward the crux of acceptance. I fully embrace it three days later, back in Brooklyn. I've returned through snow, sleet, and the same ten pop songs played on thirty different stations in an economy-class rental car with the handling of a child's tricycle.

I take the A train to the Uptown 4 to Union Square, for a

Monday movie to clear my mind. I walk from the last car to the first, scanning the faces of night crawlers like me. A Latin couple canoodles in an orange double seat. A thirty-something postal worker snores like a grizzly, his body limp against the side of the rustling train.

The train itself is an elderly arthritic, rickety and trembling as it crawls through the city's digestive tract. But it gets me where I need to go, though at the time I feel as if I'm going nowhere.

I am bringing in too little money for too much work that there isn't enough of to go around. I have spent four years in New York, but it isn't the place I had dreamed of. It is no longer a creative haven for anything.

I have chased rappers and actors, penned meaningless articles about records and films that, once published, went straight to the can at the curb. A third of my expected life had melted away and that was all I had to show for it. I could've been hit by a car the very next day, or had my brain skewered by a stray bullet, or been stabbed for the Guess brand watch my lady had given me for my twenty-sixth birthday. So little time on this earth and yet nothing was guaranteed. My grandfather had climbed the stairs to take his nightly bath one night and had come out with a sheet over his face. Still, at almost eighty-four, he'd lived a long life. And at least he had something solid to show for it.

husband

1

"You must not have blinds at your house," my grandma Sally Helen Langley chuckles, her eighty-two years of benevolence wrapped in a housedress adorned with blue and white flowers. I have to struggle with the aging string before the metal slats twist open, forcing freshly squeezed sunlight into the newly redecorated abode.

It's been nine months since my grandfather's passing and things in their house are in even better order than before. There are new cabinets in the railroad-style kitchen and a new silver fridge complete with an ice maker. The walls are now white instead of their previous lime green. The old brown carpet has been stripped away for a new burgundy one, and the green velvet couch set, a sacred cow in Langley home entertainment, has been switched out for a crème sofa and loveseat set, both with more pillows than they should be able to hold.

"There's so many pillows that when people come in to sit down they can't find nowhere to sit," she says as she smiles, taking a seat across from me. "Before he passed Jesse said he was gonna fix this place up real nice and put a sign out front that say 'The Langleys.' He had started doing everything. But he didn't finish nothin' he started. Poor thing."

Her words make me remember a visit I made to see the Lone Ranger while she was down in Richmond, VA, taking care of her sister Rebecca as she lived out her last days with cancer. There wasn't a light on in the front of the house and the dining room table was covered with two boxes full of tools. The old man had work to do.

He'd refitted the wood paneling on the first-level porch and started to build a barbecue pit in the rear yard. It was as if he was trying to keep busy, hoping that constant movement might slow the inevitable.

"Granddaddy gonna be goin' away soon," he told me. "I ain't gonna be here much longer."

I blew it off as one of his usual rants, empty words strung together just to fill the silence, or to make me laugh, or just so that he could have something to say to the grandson he barely knew.

"You're gonna be here when I got grandkids," I snapped back, feeling the awkwardness in the air. Our eyes met for a moment. We both knew that I was lying. That little exchange rang in my ears on that Monday morning, December 30, 2002, when I first got my mother's message that he had crossed over.

On this visit to their house months later, my uncle Gary is

sitting in the dining room watching music videos on BET while his mother cleans and straightens her abode, as she has done nearly every morning since the day she said "I do."

"You see I moved the TV," she grins, motioning toward the oversized idiot box in the dining room. I glance and then nod.

"I said I'm gonna let 'em watch TV in there. 'Cuz they ain't comin' out here on my new sofas. I let 'em come out here and they'll get those messed up like the last one." Her *they* is general and not specific, the result of her playing hostess to hundreds of changing faces around the neighborhood since the day she and her husband moved onto Childress Street, barely a year after their first child, my mother, was born. Everybody loves Sally Helen Langley.

At this point I am just glad that she can still sit before me, that she still smiles when I put my lips to the softness of her cheek. She's always happy to see me. She likes to remind me of that day on November 20, 1975, when I came into the world. She and my uncle Tony raced nearly twenty blocks from their jobs at the C&P phone company to George Washington University Hospital.

Her husband did not meet her there. He didn't come to rejoice over the birth of the first grandchild on both sides of the family. Her face was always most visible. His presence was most felt behind the scenes.

In August of 2003, Sally was hospitalized herself, and ended up fighting for her life on a respirator. Congestive heart failure caused by water on the lungs. She nearly collapsed in my mother's car on the way home from her doctor's office.

"I've never been that sick in my whole life," she remembered. "I couldn't sit up. I couldn't move."

She spent three days on that respirator with her children all around her. I waited by the phone in Brooklyn, all of us praying to the Creator that he would not take both of them within the same spin around the sun.

Sally Langley is now the eldest living person in my life. Sitting before me, she tries to remember all she can of the Lone Ranger's story, knowing that her words are needed for the microphone held by her eldest grandson. She knows so much more about the Lone Ranger than I do. Or so I think.

"I didn't really know much about him," she admits as Gary murmurs the lyrics to Beyoncé's "Crazy in Love" in the background. Sixty years of daily interaction and her answer comes in three short sentences. "He was real quiet. He kept to himself. Kept a lot inside."

For more than eighty years his introversion closed him off from almost everyone he knew, but it didn't stop him from speaking his mind in that colored Pentagon lunchroom when he saw the stick of a girl whom he could've only hoped might be his wife. He was twenty-two. She was nineteen.

"You's a good little girl," he said after their initial hellos. "I can't believe your mama let you come away from home as small as you is." He smiled wide, and she, being a southern woman, knew just how to respond to a man from the same region: a little giggle with a slight batting of the eyes.

"I might be small, but I've got the age," she'd replied.

"I'm gonna marry you," he then said. " 'Cuz you're the best girl I've ever met."

His prediction came true almost as smoothly as the words came from his lips. He asked her if she wanted to go to a movie. She said yes. Thus began the chain reaction that would lead to the most common ailment of all, L-O-V-E.

But Sally Helen Smith wasn't supposed to get married, at

least not then. She'd already been accepted to Saint Paul College, not far from her hometown of Powhatan, Virginia. After she graduated from high school with "good marks," the colored school superintendent had offered her and several other female seniors the opportunity of a lifetime: travel to the city of Alexandria and work at the then newly built U.S. Pentagon. The job would be for a single year, and included room and board to be provided by the superintendent's sister. Sally Helen was supposed to stay only long enough to save some money for school, because even back then "college was expensive."

Money and men, however, had a way of changing a young girl's mind in 1940. It was a given that the right man sliding a stone onto the proper finger could make any plan shrivel up like a dream deferred. Jesse knew exactly what he was doing. And Sally, as a country girl, "knew her place."

"The other girls—Ruth, Mammie, and Gladys—they all got married too," she explained. "Gladys wasn't so lucky though. Her husband used to beat on her. I don't know why she stayed. 'Cuz that's somethin' I never woulda stood for."

"Grandma Sally" was born the second youngest of ten children in the Smith clan. Her mother, Lucy Smith, was a slender woman with peanut-butter skin and a set of prominent cheekbones she passed on to her daughter. Lucy smoked a pipe until the day she died and would have a little gin with whomever joined her on the porch after sundown. Her husband, Robert Young Smith, was fair-skinned and quiet, kind but firm, a farmer who worked his piece of land until the work was done, raising his six sons to live off the land.

The girls—Sally, Rebecca, Adele, and Alean—milked cows, fixed meals, and kept house, learning from their mother all the skills needed to be the kind of woman a "good" man would want to marry. God-fearing folk, they all walked to nearby Mt. Pero Baptist Church on the two or three Sundays a month when church was held. Back then, preachers often had multiple congregations with many miles between them, and they served each on alternating Sundays during the month. Sally still brings as much of the family as she can back to Powhatan on the first Sunday in August, the day designated for homecoming at Mt. Pero, on the grounds of which her parents and siblings are buried.

Sally is one of only two Smith children who have yet to pass on. Her sister Rebecca crossed over in the summer of '02; her brother Alfred (better known as "Big Baby") in early '03; and her younger sister Alean in the summer of '04. Her oldest brothers, Richard, Levi, and Collie, have been dead for many years. Her older brother Porter, however, still lives and farms in Powhatan. Her sister Adele remains unaccounted for, lingering in the unknown by not having kept in touch.

By the time her father died in 1934, Sally was working part-time for a white family in Ballsville, just a few miles down the red dirt road from where she lived. She cooked all the meals, cleaned the chicken coop, and made more white and fluffy biscuits than she would ever want to count, all for a single dollar a week, which was less than minimum wage even back in the '30s.

"They got mad because I wouldn't wax the floors too," she said with disdain. "So I quit." The family, three kids born from a white father and Indian mother, had gotten a little beside themselves for her tastes. "I had to speak up for myself, you know?"

What she doesn't speak of are the things she'd rather not remember. The Black man she knew who was gunned down at the local gas station for allegedly saying something suggestive to a white woman. She doesn't mention the stories recounted in hushed conversations with her bedridden cousin Lucille and the wheelchair-ridden cousin Elsie, the first woman I'd ever seen with amputated legs.

I remember being nine or ten and listening to the three of them. The room smelled of bedpans and weak disinfectant as the trio spoke of young Black men being set on fire, and of people who spoke their mind against the white faces "disappearing."

She rarely talks about the family home burning down, allegedly caused by her brother Collie's not-so-steady fingers with a lit cigarette. She doesn't hint at being bothered by the fact that her mother, "Gran Lucy," lived out the last of her days in a rented house on white people's land. And she doesn't speak of her abandoned dream of building a new home on the old Smith land, one that will overshadow the shack her brother Porter has built on a mere sliver of those acres.

That's because Powhatan is a world behind her. She put old family and friends to the rear when she moved to the nation's capital, sealing them in the plastic of the past the minute she became a good man's wife, the minute she had a family of her own. Sure she sent letters home and made phone calls. Sure she visited when people were sick or when someone passed away.

But that little town was no longer her home in the same way. She no longer dressed up with all the others to thrash the wheat on the Fourth of July because fireworks and sound systems were far beyond her people's price range. She no longer sat on screenless porches until the fireflies became the only light for miles. Those things were no longer her life, nor were they the stuff of her girlhood dreams.

———

"I was always a really good seamstress," she declares. "That was what I wanted to go to school for. I wanted to move to Paris and make dresses."

For most Black folks, the capital of France was a world away. But my grandma saw it in her mind every night she spent in the sewing classes she took after work during the first few years of her marriage.

"I only had a few more classes to go when Jesse told me that he wanted me to stop," she tells me. "He said that he didn't want me to be in school anymore. So I stopped, because I knew that that was what a good wife was supposed to do. You didn't argue or make any problems where there didn't need to be any. But I don't think I was really ready to be married and have children. I still regret not finishing that school, even until this day."

Sally had been raised to be a "good wife." And in her time, good wives didn't rock the boat. If your husband wanted something, you did it. If a sacrifice on the wife's part made a household better, you did it. Because at the end of the day your man was doing the hard part. He was the provider. He was keeping the bills paid. Thus, what he wanted always came first.

Jesse, despite his demands, did his best to be a good husband, even if he often contradicted himself. Clinging to the Good Book, the only words whose value he never questioned, he wanted his wife to be a Sarah to his Abraham, unmoved in her love and willing to bend toward his every whim. Sally was definitely it.

"As soon as we got married he told me that he didn't want me to work anymore," she says. "He wanted me to stay at home and take care of the house while he went to work. But

I guess he wasn't making enough at first to really do that. Because six months later he was telling me, 'You better get out there and get you a job.' "

But none of that meant that he didn't love Sally Helen. And he went out of his way to show that in the beginning. When she was working as an elevator operator at Garfinckel's department store in downtown DC, Jesse would travel from his post-Pentagon job unloading freight cars, just to have lunch with his lady. He would do the same later on when he began driving trucks for the Embassy Dairy. Every day at noon, his truck could be found in front of the Langley house as he sat inside and ate the meal she had made for him.

"He acted like he was supposed to back then in the beginning," she remembers. "He'd take me to dances from time to time and go with me to church every Sunday. One time he bought me a gray mutton coat from the furrier downtown that cost $298. That was right before he took me down to Greenville for the first time after we got married. Everybody wanted to touch that coat. We even used to go fishing together. And after the kids were born he used to take us all for a drive every Sunday."

But along the way something began to change in him, and then in their union. It was something that Sally can't seem to pinpoint. As the kids grew, the hugs and kisses decreased. Spousal hands no longer clasped. The mutton coat dried out and browned on a hanger in the basement. The wedding rings were stolen and all but forgotten.

The words between them became fewer and fewer, replaced by pulls on his cigarettes and lips pursed around bottles filled with fiery fluid. Jesse found more and more solace beneath the hood of his car, and less in the room where

A young Sally and Jesse, back when "he acted right."

his children were conceived. Then one day, for no identifiable reason, he told Sally Helen that he was moving out of their bedroom and into the guest room at the other end of the top floor.

"I begged him not to," she says. "I begged him to talk to me about it. But he had made his mind up. And that was that."

No one seems to know (or is willing to tell me) when or how it happened, or the reasons. The rest of the family just dealt with things as they came in the decades that followed. Christmas dinners with the patriarch eating in the kitchen, sipping on a blend of eggnog so potent that it could've started a car. Out of the blue Jesse would hurl sharpened words at the woman everyone loved to love. There were no more anniversary celebrations. Not as many Sunday drives. Just paid bills and the deed for a home in the Langley name.

There are photographs from years long gone of my grandparents smiling wide, holding each other tightly in marital bliss, hints of a life less solemn, a life that was long gone by the time I entered the world. But good times did flash through every now and again.

On Sally Helen's eighty-first birthday, my mother and uncles rented a white stretch limo to take her to a seafood dinner. We all dressed up for the occasion, sipping on the cold soda that replaced the champagne that would've come with the deal, because my grandma doesn't drink.

The driver, complete with hat and gloves, rolled a red carpet from the family porch all the way to the open automobile door. And my grandfather appeared to take her hand and walk her all the way there. But he wouldn't go with us. He never went with us.

"I miss him now more than I did when he was here," my grandmother admits. "That last night he came in the kitchen

Jesse, near the end, on the stroll with his number one lady.

and told me, 'Gimme some chicken out of that pan.' He always liked to eat out of the pan whenever I cooked. And I told him, 'Jesse, I'ma fix you a plate. Sit down there an' eat.' And he ate, then he got up and started out of the kitchen. Then he said to me, 'Sally, you sure done got ugly. If I had known you was gonna get that ugly, I wouldn't have married you.' And I said back, 'Jesse, when was the last time you looked in the mirror?' It had gotten to the point where when he said anything like that it just tickled me. It didn't bother me anymore."

Then he walked out into the living room where my mother was sitting. He looked his only daughter right in the eye and said, "Angie, I tease your mama like that. But I love her." Then he went up to take a bath.

"Next thing I knew Gary was dragging him out the tub and the ambulance came. If I had known that he was teasing before I would've been more affectionate to him. But I guess I know now that he acted the way he did because he didn't know how to show his feelings. I always felt sorry for him because of that. Maybe that's why I stayed with him all the way until the end."

I'm not sure that it was all teasing. A marriage is not that second-grade boy-girl game where he hits you because he likes you, or at least it shouldn't be. And I'm definitely not sure that my grandmother became completely immune to her husband's words, even though she'll swear otherwise until the day she joins him on the other side. I think that his tongue lashed because he always envied her, because he wished that everyone would love him the way they loved her, and that he could embrace their smiles and stories, that he could salve broken hearts and make his children happy in the way that only she could.

I think he saw in her all that he was not, and he kept her close with the hope that her light might shine into the places that much of his early life had left empty. But at the end of the day it didn't turn out as well as he'd hoped. He was left with a lifetime of knowing her warmth and beauty, but never fully feeling it for himself.

Almost a year has passed since his death and my grand-mother is still more of a wife than a widow. Though she no longer rises as early in the day, she still cooks and cleans house as much as she can, taking it easy when her still-healing body tells her she's pushed herself too far. All of her children have moved beyond the house on Childress Street, save Gary.

Both mother and remaining resident son still expect to see the man of the house, often finding themselves waiting to hear those slow, heavy steps coming down the creaking stair-case. Faint traces of tobacco and his Polo cologne still hang in the air. That's all that remains for a pair of his greatest devo-tees to hold on to.

Sally Helen doesn't know what to do now that he's gone. My mother comes to the house every other day, to help her write the checks for bills, to supervise the ceaseless remodel-ing that began in the summer months, and to make sure she gets outside the house every once in a while.

When I was a boy you needed a tracking device to pin-point Sally Helen's position in the world. She was always on the move. She took shopping trips with old friends and walks around the block, or she'd ride the bus downtown to do some window-shopping. Those friends have passed on, and win-dows full of clothes just don't mean what they used to.

Her world has become the three floors she owns on Chil-dress Street, as if she is somehow enslaved by the spirit of her departed partner. Sure it wasn't no fairy tale. But they made it last. The kids grew up and they grew old. God spared them from cancer, strokes, and heart attacks even though they put away more fried food and lard than the current generation could ever swallow. Sometimes I think that Sally Helen Langley feels there's nothing left, that she feels old, even though she could pass for sixty. Without him, nothing is the same. It seems like she's just waiting for her turn to go home.

2

Angela is an obvious derivative of *angel,* and it is the angels, soldiers of the Lord, who bring about many of the Creator's miracles. Following suit, it was Angela Marilyn Langley who brought the hope that her parents, then in their late twenties, might be able to live up to the Old Testament's mandate to "be fruitful and multiply." She was the first child to enter Sally Helen and Jesse's world whole, after two miscarriages and a boy who didn't live past sixty days.

I can only imagine the joy they must have felt to see that pretty girl fresh from the birth canal, her lungs filled with air, her eyes straining to take in the light of a brave new world.

Sally Helen and Jesse showed young Angela that marriage wasn't necessarily about love. It was about being there, and staying there. As a spouse you were supposed to deal with your partner's differences in whatever area of life. You made it through the good and the not so good. True love was about putting the other person first.

Born on October 22, 1949, Angela was the only Langley child to remember life in the small home her parents rented before they bought the house at 1341 Childress Street. She excelled in her studies and won a copy of Stephen Crane's *The Red Badge of Courage* as her prize in a school competition. As the oldest, it was she who shepherded her younger brothers through the neighborhood until it was safe for them to move around on their own. And, perhaps most important, she was the first of the four to marry and have a child, me.

Mom as a baby, with Sally.

My mama was the one who never rocked the boat, the one all could depend on to make sure things got done. It was her name that was added to her father's bank accounts, just in case something happened to him. And now she's the one who travels to the family home nearly every other day—even though Uncle Gary still lives there—to make sure that her mother is getting along in the absence of the family's one and only provider.

My mother, like her mother, is still in mourning, even though more than a year has passed since Jesse died. Weeks before this interview, she relived the loss all over again when she was presented with a framed photograph of herself and her father. Her eyes welled with tears, with nothing but pride keeping them from spilling over.

"My father showed me that a husband is a provider and the head of the household, the central figure in the family," my mother says. "He bears the most responsibility, for his wife, and for his children. He always felt that the male should be the only one responsible where having a job was concerned. He was never happy when my mother was working."

Even now I don't think she would ever describe her parents' relationship as abusive. To her, he just showed love in a different way. Anything he might have said meant nothing in light of what he did for the family: the Sunday drives through the city and into the deepest reaches of the surrounding suburbs, the money he provided for full meals for all each and every night. He helped her go to college. He found a new engine for her '88 Corsica after the old one broke down right in front of the U.S. Capitol while I was at the wheel. Her daddy was always there for her. He always provided.

As Jesse's "papoose," she always strove to set an example, avoiding liquor and cigarettes, and even boyfriends, for most of her adolescence. She kept her head in the books and kept working toward her dream: teaching. My mother earned her BA in education from what was then Cheyney State College and thus became the only one of her father's children to graduate from an institution of higher learning.

Genetics gave her her mother's peanut-butter skin and stature, as well as a powerful sense of intuition about people, particularly children. She feels it when things are wrong. She knows when a child is hindered or not doing his best. Getting children back on track is what drives her more than anything else, sometimes to a fault.

Teaching was one of the most honorable professions in the world of Sally Helen and the Lone Ranger. The ability to educate was particularly prized in the rural southern communities from which they came, places where being taught about anything beyond labor or crops was as rare as finding a four-leaf clover.

Yet somewhere between high school and college, Angela

was infected with the same bug that took her mother down a generation before. She fell in love with a boy from the neighborhood, a handsome young man with a gift for art, a nice boy whose family Sally Helen had known since their children had attended the same kindergarten. The boy's name was Melvin Jasper, Jr., or "Jazz," as he was known around the way.

Melvin was everything she could have hoped for. He was funny and polite, courteous and creative. At five eleven with a big frame, he had brown eyes with an almost Asian look. When there was beef around the way he didn't want any part of, he spent the whole day at the local library. When "The Movement" came along, he sprouted his 'fro and organized and protested, threatening local white businessmen who took advantage of their Black patrons. He was strong, like her father, which meant that when it came to Angela's heart, resistance was futile.

It was so long ago that neither remembers exactly how it happened. They were both in college, both traveling their chosen paths. He drove from DC to Cheyney practically every weekend. She told him that she loved him and he felt the same. They were two beautiful Black people at the end of the '60s. The possibilities were endless, or at least they seemed to be. Getting married was the only thing that made sense, the only remaining bridge for them to cross.

"I never really thought about the characteristics I wanted in a

Jazz and Angie on New Year's, 1972.

husband, or what a marriage itself entailed," she tells me. "I hadn't had any other relationships of substance besides him. Plus I was still in college. And in college it was the thing to get engaged and have a ring on your finger. I didn't think about setting goals about what I wanted in a relationship. At the time my choices had a lot more to do with Melvin's philosophy about life, both personal and political. And we had fun spending time together."

Wearing a white dress topped off with a veiled African head wrap, she said "I do" before the altar at the Bethesda Baptist Church on Mount Olivet Road in Northeast DC, the very same church where the two had attended Sunday school together. Her father gave her away. The groom and his boys donned velvet dashikis with embroidered collars. It was 1971.

"My mother and I never really talked about the duties of a wife. But I observed throughout my life what she did. I learned that as a wife, you cook and clean and iron and prepare food. I also saw that she was always very hospitable. She always considered others and wanted people to come by the house to have a nice meal."

But Sally Helen was from a different era. It was the '70s when Angela married and adulthood was in the midst of drastic change. With a background in special education, she found a position teaching blind teenagers at the Jackson Center for the Visually Impaired in Georgetown. But, surprisingly, it was not the students but the parents and administrators who made the job very difficult. So much jealousy and infighting, backbiting and deceit. At an institution designed to help seeds grow, some people were unwittingly strangling them.

Things weren't much different for Melvin. He was a firstyear grad student at American University studying economics and working a retail job he hated. He was struggling through it all, trying to parlay a perceived risk-free career that would suppress the artist in him. The world wasn't what either of them had expected.

Sally Helen hadn't warned her daughter that it was a jungle out there, because she didn't know. It was no longer as simple as being wife and provider. It wasn't as simple as working at the job and not bringing the stress home to the family. Teaching children wasn't like driving a truck filled with milk, and Melvin wanted more from his partner than dinner and a freshly pressed uniform.

"I couldn't follow my mother's example in my own marriage. I tried, and I was very good at some of those things. But it was always difficult for me to manage my professional responsibilities. I was always bringing what happened at work home, because of my deep commitment and calling to do what I did. There were a lot of things I internalized that I really shouldn't have. I wasn't as consistent as I should have been." In her mind it was always her fault. She always assumed that she was to blame. She wasn't working hard enough. She wasn't on time. She hadn't taken on enough of the load at work.

It was safer to adopt that philosophy than to accept how much better she was at the job than all the rest of them. Thus, she brought it all across the threshold, even when she didn't mean to. And Melvin often bore the brunt of what was left over.

"I had more opportunities to be myself in my marriage than in the one my parents had, and to do what I wanted to do. Melvin and I shared a lot of the responsibilities. In some things he was just better than I was anyway. He supported my dreams and encouraged me to make them happen."

Different, however, did not necessarily mean better. I was

born exactly four years after their wedding day. And with a child, things changed. Numbers had to be crunched. Schedules and timetables became serious issues.

Having abandoned careers as both an architectural draftsman and an economist, my dad decided he wanted to make his way in the growing field of graphic design, which worked out well when he was hired into a salaried position at the DC Department of Housing. But when he went out on his own as a freelancer, and the money did not arrive consistently in the form of a check every other week, voices rose and doors began to slam. Mom wasn't used to being the primary provider. That wasn't the way she'd seen things growing up.

They both worked as I grew. Little Kenji learned to crawl and then walk. I split my chin on a curb at two and had to have stitches while my mama looked on hysterically. I won school awards and was placed in "gifted and talented" programs. I was their pride and joy, their greatest success, their individual bests blended into a little boy with his mother's fingers and father's big skull. To this day, their roles as my parents were probably the only thing they got right on the very first try.

The Jasper Family: Volume 1—Dad, Mom, and me.

"The biggest trial in a marriage is when the two of you see each other pulling apart or going in different directions. You'd love for things to be the way they used to be. But things are different. You're beginning to form different ideas and concepts about things. You change. And that's the biggest trial, staying together and growing together, despite the changes in vocation, or beliefs, etcetera."

My father did not believe in God. The tragic death of a close friend in a motorcycle accident had robbed him of his faith before he was fourteen. This posed a sizable problem for my mother. But she loved him, and he was willing to allow her to give his son to her religion. Still, there were silent questions at the New Macedonia Baptist Church, and a feeling of absence when she and I clasped hands to pray in the smallest bedroom of 3807A W Street SE, while he was in the other room.

I was six or seven when the questions congealed in my mind. Why didn't Dad come to church? Why did he keep his eyes open during grace? Why weren't we one of those blessed Christian families the late Pastor Lee Walls referred to that "prayed together and stayed together"?

Money, religion, and gender roles. Who would have thought that the love between a man and a woman couldn't be enough? Who would've known that the cultural ideal of getting hitched and staying that way had to do with so much more than L-O-V-E?

Things fell apart. More and more plays failed to earn the needed first down. They were young and still learning about themselves. Angela had learned that marriage meant staying together until the end, no matter what. Melvin had seen the same thing in his own home, and he swore to himself that he would never live or love the way his parents had.

Much later I would learn that almost all of it was about money. Someone spent too much. Someone else didn't spend enough. Mom couldn't leave the strain of work at the front door, but had no problem chiding my father about his short-comings. Dad wanted to stay more than anything, not just for me, or for the family. My mother was the love of his life, the woman he'd pledged to be with forever. Yet he was having migraines so awful that he had to lie still in the dark just to be able to endure the anguish.

I could never sleep during the arguments. The condo seemed so small, though it was the largest unit in the building. I would lie flat on my stomach by the closed door to my room and try to listen. Her voice would go from alto to shrill soprano. His voice would take on an icy detachment unlike any I've ever heard to this day. Then he'd be off into the night in search of something to stave off the inevitable, something he never managed to find.

In the end, they drafted their own joint custody agreement so that I could know my father the way both of them had known their own. A U-Haul came. He left and she stayed. It was over, though it would take more than a decade for her to see it that way.

She has never said it, but I know she viewed my father's departure as the worst kind of failure on her part. Here she was, the firstborn child of a man and a woman who had made it through poverty and inferior education, through being Black and leaving all they'd known in hopes of finding something better, and through four children—all the while being diametrically opposed personalities. Her parents had made it through more than thirty years of marriage and she'd barely gotten a third of the way with a man who was everything her father wasn't.

After my father left, she retreated from the world, working until she collapsed, her frame swaddled in a lime-green blanket coated in lint, taking in as much television as she could stand. She couldn't forgive herself for failing. She couldn't believe that "'till death do us part" had been nullified by a hidden clause in the contract known as irreconcilable differences.

"If I had to do it all over again, I definitely would not have married right out of college, to go straight from my parents' home to being a wife. I would've waited, because that had a lot to do with the difficulties I had."

It took more than a decade for her to recover from the divorce, a lot of shopping and sleeping and working herself to the bone. She slumbered through the alarm many mornings, leaving me to make sure she awoke before I went off to school.

She didn't know what to do in the wake of separation. Everything she had observed about being an adult required two people, not one. To make it worse, Melvin couldn't always handle his financial end, though he tried. She felt like she'd gotten a raw deal, that he got off lightly for leaving her.

The whole world was conspiring against her, even her own son, the boy who carried her ex-husband's face, who'd inherited his build and sense of humor. She was raising a younger version of the man she wished she could get over. It was hard.

The fights between us were excuses for what lay beneath. There was the pair of pants she threw at my face because they hadn't been ironed well enough for church, the yelling matches over my struggles with complex mathematics, and my inability not to ask questions, not to always have a better alternative to doing or fixing something than she might have had. Melvin's ghost haunted us until I left home at seventeen, fleeing the proverbial nest to do that thing called finding myself.

Mom, Dad, and I at my Morehouse baccalaureate in 1997.

The wounds began to heal via collegiate phone lines and holiday visits. She was always worried that I'd make the same mistakes that she and Dad had. The raised voices and biting threats were often the only way she knew to express her love for me. She'd seen that kind of love from someone else, from the man who called her "papoose."

She was forced to move on when Melvin remarried. There were no more excuses once her son went off to college. She cut her perm and went natural again. She became more involved in her church and moved out of the home she and Melvin had once found together. And at fifty-six, she has lived to tell the tale.

"I don't think the nature of relationships has changed between my parents' time and mine. Love is love. Your material status may change. Your professional status may change. But love doesn't change, and your faith and trust in one another in a marriage shouldn't change."

She wants me to get married, so that she can have herself some grandkids. But only if it's with a woman I truly love, a woman I can spend the rest of my life with, whom I'll never think of leaving, because she's everything I've ever dreamt of. Even then, she knows that my road may be more difficult than her own.

"In terms of the current generation, there are so many more opportunities available to them. They can experience diversity in every area of their lives, from their education and professional life to their personal experiences. But I think they are a little bit impatient. For them, relationships are really not valued. They don't really stick things out. But a part of that is that nowadays you really don't have to. My fear is that there won't be a lot of marriage. Because in this particular generation, marriage is not a priority.

"A lot of people are doing this thing where they want to move in together and try things out. The world itself has made it very easy for people to think about not marrying. But I hope that despite the political and legal changes, that those things continue to be a priority in the people that seek long-time commitments."

It's not too late for her to think about remarrying either. Men her age ask about the woman in the photo at my apartment. It ain't over 'til it's over; it's always OK to start again.

"He'd have to be saved," she begins her list of requirements for a man. "And funny, and respectful, and love children, and . . ."

When the list is full she feels as if she hasn't said enough. She always wants to teach a complete lesson, never leaving anything out, all *i*'s dotted and *t*'s crossed, no accents out of place. She's still her father's child. She still wants everything perfect. She still has to have it her way.

3

Things rarely stop moving in my father's house. Melvin Jasper, Jr., is the only male to offset his second wife, Carla, their two daughters, Annia, thirteen, and Imani, twelve, and a two-year-old female Labrador named Diva. No longer a graphic artist, he now pays the bills as a real estate appraiser, still making his own days and hours, and still working well into the night, every night, like he's still young and hungry.

Annia, the slightly older and chattier of my two stepsisters, announces that some pot pies are ready in the kitchen. He has to stop talking to thank her before he can continue. As I said, things around there never stop moving.

My father now lives more than half an hour from the borders of the city he used to love, the place he showed me inside out with nothing but a few dollars and a subway card for each of us. There wasn't a museum I didn't see, nor a restaurant where we didn't dine. He taught me the Metro subway system before I was eight, but still secretly followed me on my route to school the first few times, just to make sure I was safe.

He would always tell me that DC was the town for Black people, the symbol of us governing ourselves and thus the mascot for Black Nationalism. For a child of the '60s this meant everything, and he wanted me, then his only child, to live with an understanding of that importance. Though I'm decades older and four hours away, it's something I've never forgotten.

"It's like that old Bible verse," he says. "When I was a child I saw things as a child. It was pretty much Mom and Dad and happy family. When I looked at my parents it occurred to me that both of these people had taken on different responsibilities, for me. My father was out working to provide for us and my mother was at home taking care of me and the house."

But as he got older my dear ole dad started to catch the fissures in his folks' marital facade. They were always yelling and bickering, mostly about money, and it affected him quite a bit. Some might even say it scarred him.

As the years went on he discovered that he was seeing only the tip of the iceberg, that "there was all kinds of acrimony going on." His father "was no saint." He smoked a pack of Marlboros a day and chased them with Crown Royal and Teacher's scotch and took his time coming home after work. Things between husband and wife were functional, never warm and cozy, but functional.

He was determined that wasn't the way his marriage was going to be. He refused to reprise his father's role as the tortured provider, as the man of the house who often found himself more imprisoned than enamored by his responsibilities as a husband. Money would never be that important to him. He'd never allow it to create that cloud of tension or disharmony that always seemed to be hanging over his parents' relationship.

He told me he'd never marry again after he and my mother split. He'd make his own home for the two of us, a place where we could both grow and prosper. But in the beginning that "place" was transitory. His first solo spot was an apartment on Capitol Hill's Tenth Street, the next a fold-out sofa in his parents' basement in Benning Heights. Then, finally, he got his first home as a single man, a two-bedroom in Temple Hills, Maryland, that he renovated with the help of me and his second-wife-to-be.

Like my mother, it took him nearly a decade to truly get his bearings after the divorce. There were many nights out in the streets while I slept. Empty interludes in places where the phone rang once time was up. He had married Angela for forever. But forever, as he would say, "was not in the cards."

"Marriage is a complicated arrangement between a man and a woman that can't be too rigid, that always has to have room at the margins, some give for each person to be able to say or do or retreat to their own little fortress of solitude to regroup. My mother's fortress was being able to shop and spend and indulge. For my father, it was work. He liked the guys he worked with and the guys he served with in the reserves. He liked having family gatherings. And those were the areas where they remained apart from each other, while keeping the marriage together.

"I don't know how well it worked out though. I never thought that they were really suited for each other. Sure, they had both come from similar places in terms of their own backgrounds, and even though they annoyed each other tremendously sometimes, they were also very resilient as a couple. They actually had one of the longest sustained marriages of the people they knew in their generation."

Between his parents there never seemed to be an outward expression of a romantic love for one another. The household was a business and they ran it as partners, assuming their God-given roles and playing them with zeal until the curtain fell at the end of each evening. That was all they had, similar values and backgrounds and an established rhythm of keeping the wheels turning. There was never chemistry between them.

"I knew that I didn't want to be in a marriage like the one I saw them living through, so I'm not."

When my mother, Angela, was growing up in the house on Childress Street, Melvin, Jr., was living with his parents and younger brother, Michael, in an apartment a few blocks away on Simms Place. His future wife had been a familiar face since childhood, as had the rest of her family. The neighborhood was so tightly knit that many of their childhood friends also ended up together. Leslie married Janice. Rodney got with Loretta, and Joe snagged Belinda.

Everybody knew each other between Trinidad Avenue and Holbrook Street. The Jaspers and the Langleys were no exception.

"There were a lot of similarities between my parents' marriage and the one Sally and Jesse had, even though my parents were about nine years younger. They were both Black families who sustained themselves by a lot of hard work and staked out a working-class life for their families when that was not an easy thing for Black people to do. Both men were blue-collar workers and the mothers were pretty much stay-at-home mothers.

"There were differences too, though, because my parents grew up urbanites, even though their roots were in the country. So, because the Langleys were more rural in their upbringing, they tended to be a little more circumspect and less forthcoming with their opinions in mixed company."

Though there was a certain kind of tension between them, Melvin was always respectful to Jesse in the years he was courting Angela. Much of the conflict centered on Jesse's attitude toward his own household, which was very different from what young "Jazz" was used to.

"My father had more opportunities to find and express himself than Jesse did," my father says. "He was a standout athlete and achieved a lot of notoriety and attention from his ability to play different sports as a young man. And he was more of a man's man. He went to the military and worked his way up from being a buck private to a first sergeant. At his job, he went from a porter to a driver to being a leader of all the drivers.

"Jesse had been raised by his grandparents, which meant that he got an even more conservative upbringing than his contemporaries. And that made him much more patriarchal. My father came from a broken home. So he grew up as the oldest male child who had to assume responsibilities for the house and for the care and protection of his family. He had to learn to do things like cook and do housework and take care of his younger brothers and sisters as well as make money to bring home. So for him, when he had his own family, it wasn't a question of creating the kind of patriarchy that Jesse had.

"In our house everybody wore different hats. Even though my father was the breadwinner, he enjoyed cooking on the weekends. He liked going to the market and buying the food for the meals, which I rarely saw Jesse do."

In the story of the Black neighborhood, there are always those who stay, who remain within the blocks and corners where they were born, and those who escape, those whose dreams cannot be restrained by such boundaries. Melvin, Angela, and a handful of their friends were the ones who chose to follow the path away from Trinidad. Many of the rest remain in the neighborhood, to this day.

After a few months of studying to be a draftsman, Jazz

went on to study economics at Federal City College, where he received his BS before going into a master's program at American University, which he did not finish. Art was the thing that always moved him. Even as kids he and his best friend Rodney would draw their own comic books on regular paper, scripting their own stories just to pass the time.

He'll never forget the first time he saw his first future wife. They were both about ten years old. It was a spring day in the fifth grade and she was across the street from her house at the neighborhood rec center, twirling her baton along with a dozen other aspiring majorettes for the center's cheering squad.

It just so happened that they both went to Crummell Elementary School together, and then Brown Junior High, and then Eastern High School. Their names came close on the weekly roll at Bethesda Baptist Church's Sunday school. They flashed smiles and shared the occasional neighborhood gossip. He walked her home from the playground when it was getting dark.

But they were just friends. They never kissed, never touched, or even held hands until well after high school was over and they crossed paths again at the sandwich stand on the corner of Sixteenth and L during their second year of college. They exchanged numbers and he made the call. And she, in turn, called him back.

He was up at Cheyney every other weekend to visit. Love was something neither of them had ever expected. She was two months into her first teaching gig when the two of them jumped the broom, the both of them just barely twenty-two.

"I didn't think about the requirements for being a husband until I was married," my father says. "But one of the things my pop taught me that always stuck about marriage was accept-

Mom and Dad's wedding.

ing differences between the two of you and not reacting to them unless they were major.

"Once Angela and I had a falling out about something and I remember telling him that I didn't understand her. And he told me that I would never completely understand women. They're different from men and the thing to keep in mind is how important those differences are in the whole scheme of things. Is it serious enough to destroy the family, or is it just something that rubs you the wrong way? If it's very important, then it's something you have to deal with. If it's minor, then you let it go.

"And there was never this hard and fast rule about what was men's work or women's work. It was never that kind of crap in our house. My father would cook and wax the floors. He did whatever was good for the household as a whole."

Still, such advice could only do so much good with what Mel, Jr., was dealing with. My paternal granddad had come to accept marriage as an exercise in tolerance, a collaboration as opposed to a coexistence, but my father wanted only to love and be loved in return. Sure he wanted to raise kids and build a family in the way his father had, living as part of a unit where everyone had a responsibility, where all had work to do. But he also wanted to do it in his own way, and with someone who respected his particular game plan.

But going into the '80s, the business of freelance graphic art was topsy-turvy at best. Working out of the family apartment, it was feast or famine. And when the checks were late, or not there at all, there was little he could do beyond hoping for a reprieve in the months to follow. Angela's salary was the raft that kept the clan afloat. That didn't make her happy, and the effect of her unhappiness took its toll on him. He was caught in the same trap that had snared his father. But unlike his father before him, my dear old dad decided to gnaw himself out.

The work never stopped fluctuating in the decade that followed. The T square and X-Acto knife gave way to the mouse and the Macintosh. Then he lost interest in the business. Real estate appraisal became the new game, around the same time that the recession hit. Interest rates and the competition were against him. The bank foreclosed on his first home and he lost almost everything in it.

Along the way he met another woman, younger and more aggressive, one who suited him in different ways. They had two girls and found a new house. Then came two cars and the dog, and a second chance at the African American dream.

"Marriage is very different from one household to the

next. What works for one couple won't work for another. That's the way it should be. Couples negotiate what works for them over time.

"The greatest challenge is making the relationship broad enough to fulfill what both parties need. That both husband and wife get from it what they need to get from it, plus a little more. Your partner needs to be your sanctuary, a confidante, a best friend, a partner in life. Often, from what I've seen, that's not the case. When people have a genuine friendship and respect for that other person in addition to the love they feel, then they have a real good chance of sustaining the marriage. And what they can't supply for themselves is there from their spouse."

His ideals have changed since the '60s struggles. An American flag has hung on his porch since 9/11. He supported sending troops into Afghanistan and Iraq. Geographically he was a stone's throw away from the plane that hit the Pentagon, and if people indiscriminately put his family's life at risk, then they have to be dealt with, no matter what color they are. If he were a young man now, he would've volunteered to go and fight. Yet when he was a young man in the '60s he got a student deferment to stay out of Vietnam.

"My generation was hung up on self-fulfillment. For us, it was about finding your own self and being what you wanted to be. This is why you had the friction about male and female roles, whereas you didn't have that at all in my parents' generation.

"With my parents, getting married was what was expected. The opportunities for them were more limited, in terms of both education and cultural norms. Their occupational choices were much more narrow. It was always going to be physical work for the husband, and if the wife did work, she was going to do some form of domestic or service work, unless she had gone to college.

"For us, opportunities just exploded. There were all kinds of colleges, different kinds of work that became available for you to aspire to that weren't even on the landscape in my parents' time. My father understood what a blueprint draftsman was when I went to school for it. But he had a hard time understanding what a graphic designer was, even when I brought home things to show him what I did. My favorite anecdote is the first time I went down to visit Angela's people in Powhatan, during the time I was studying to be an economist. Her uncle Porter took me around and proudly introduced me as his niece's fiancé, who was studying to be a 'communist.'

"We had so many choices that they devoured us. The families and marriages that failed didn't work because people could do whatever they wanted to do. Life was a smorgasbord, both materially and sexually. People got caught up in trying to do everything and be everything. Ultimately they became preoccupied with 'me.'

"That's why the current generation is just so ravaged by divorce, and an inability to perpetuate some sort of consistent family structure for far too many children. So for them, it's now a question of figuring out what relationships between a man and a woman are supposed to be like. What's the basis for marriage? It's no longer economic and no longer for procreation. Because now you can do both without the need for the blessing of the church or society. How does this thing work, since so few of them have actually seen it work? They only have a blueprint for transient kinds of things, what you see essentially in music videos, physical attraction for thirty seconds on the screen, and nothing else.

"The whole thing is changing. It's morphing, and this generation will have to work out what's actually needed and how they will be different from or similar to all of the relationships that have happened before."

I call my dad often to vent about my relationship woes. He tells me that I'm so much like my mother. Then I tell him that she says that I'm so much like him, just the opposite. Then we both concede that it's a matter of perception.

My father's next challenge will perhaps be his greatest: the little boys who are already chasing after his daughters. My sisters are not allowed to give out their phone number and fear strict monitoring once full-out adolescence hits.

It's another stage in the game of life, "the only game in town," as he puts it from time to time, when someone tells him that they want to quit. Life never stops being hard. But it never stops rewarding either. He raises from his recliner and turns left toward the kitchen. There are pot pies waiting.

4

The only reason for the Lone Ranger ever to enter Moe's Bar in Fort Greene would be to use the bathroom. A shy, Baptist, Bible-toting country boy like him would never have anything to do with a place like this. The redheaded barkeep wears an elaborate tattoo down her left arm. The lanky DJ fades between vinyl spinning at thirty-three revolutions per minute. Various sistas are spread across the room, both looking and not looking at whatever men, because there's nothing else better to do.

My significant other is currently on ice. A friend of more than a decade, she woke up one day and decided that she loved me. I was informed of this via a drunk dial after midnight, and I was expected to fall in line and reciprocate, even though I was with someone else at the time. In short, the old thing eventually ended and then the new thing began.

For her I was the eventuality of the equation that had been her life. A nice guy, someone who would take care of her. She was Jenny and I was Forest, the one she came home to when the lights started to go dim. She promised she'd never play me the way the others had. She promised that she could be with me forever. She promised that she wasn't going after Betty Ford's record at the open bar. Needless to say, a lot of her promises ended in pieces and I have ended up at Moe's.

Wearing one of my grandfather's coats (the Claude Berceville camel-hair number with the worn lapel), I'm two rum and Cokes in, and am wondering exactly why I'm there myself. I should be home transcribing tapes or making notes. I should be in bed. But it's too early to go home to an empty mattress, and her scent still lingers on the sheets, even after multiple cleansings.

Sleeping alone at winter's doorstep is about as desirable as gum surgery. So I'm here, running down the clock until I'm ready to collapse, wasting time and effort on legal drugs and the delusion of meaningful social interaction.

My father always tells me that I am my mother's child. This is true in a variety of ways, but most notably in one that he probably doesn't think about. I always play it safe. My pattern is to date one woman at a time. I ask them a million questions. I make sure they are educated and articulate. I choose ones who seem gentle in their own way, even if they've added a tough-girl glaze just to make themselves a little harder to read. And almost all of them have reminded me of my mother, even if it was in ways that I didn't consciously recognize.

I never met Jesse Langley, Sr.'s, mother, nor can Sally Helen, my mother, or anyone else recall her name. Even the Lone Ranger knew her only when he was a baby. So I cannot say that he chose the same way I did when he married Sally Helen. I assume, though, believing in at least some of what Freud has to say, that he probably saw something familiar in her, something that begged him to take a closer look.

When Jesse found Sally it was all so simple. As the man, he immediately started the moves toward that checkmating move called a marriage. Polite banter followed by courting followed by picking up extra shifts to afford something nice for the day he was going to broach the idea of their spending a life together. That was how it went back then.

You meet someone you love, then you slap the bracelets on them, find a home, and start cranking out kids, whom you in turn raise, respectively, to play their role in the same sort of process. It was a no-brainer.

For my parents the arrangement required a little more thought. They found their way to adulthood in a time of sweeping change. The struggles for civil rights and the sexual revolution made the air crackle with a spanking new brand of idealism. They wanted to change the world, to fight the power, to be their own men and women, and to find someone else who wanted the exact same thing.

Then they made their choices, only to find that things, and people, were a lot different once the parties and protests died down, when disco came and went, when they got Reagan in the White House. All of a sudden the people with whom they were going to change the world became just people, people who, as it turned out, they might not have known as well as they'd thought. It stopped being fun. It stopped being about ideals. And for some of them it then got a lot easier to get that public assistance check when there wasn't a man living in the house.

Husbands and wives went their own ways, most never to intersect again. The kids were left with whomever remained static, which was usually mom, and thus they had to grow up without a part of themselves, a part lost in the dying winds of change. A once-fierce gale simmered down to a breeze that eventually resulted in nothing but hard feelings and white lies told at tuck-in time, to make it all go down easier.

I am one of those children. And though my parents' marriage dissolved before I was eight years old, they were smart enough, selfless enough, to make sure that my relationships with both of them remained intact. I was shuttled back and forth between their homes in both week and weekend intervals until I was seventeen.

Still, I cannot escape the images of my father loading his things into that U-haul. I remember walking the loading ramp as if it were a tightrope, playing this shifting of furniture and boxes as if it were some kind of a game, as if things would go back to the way I'd always known them, just because I wanted them to be the way I'd always known them. I didn't know where my mother was when my father and his brother Mike sealed the truck. And I didn't know where my dad was going with all of his stuff. I got into that truck because there was no other choice.

What was one instantly became two. Two different rooms with my name on them. Two different beds and two different bus routes. Sometimes I'd forget where I was going and end up at the wrong residence. Sometimes I'd wish I didn't have to pack up everything and the dog on Friday afternoons so that I could make the switch from one to the other. Sometimes it felt as if home was only in my head, as if the warm place out of which I came existed only in my memory, because eventually I was all that remained to prove that my parents' marriage had happened at all.

These images have become more familiar than any sense of permanent union. The designated family room is used for storage. Everyone in the family eats dinner somewhere else. The kid you've known since kindergarten snaps after being extorted by one bully too many and opens fire on a room full of the elderly at the nursing home where he works. The president of your daughter's PTA is dealing weed out of the school snack bar, and the company you work for cuts a thousand jobs just so they can hold their quarterly retreat in Cancún instead of Canton, Ohio.

We are Chicken Littles with the heartfelt feeling that the sky is falling all around us. Our solution is to get money and all the material things we can so that we'll have something to brag about to our friends right before Armageddon. We come out of the womb as cynics, our faces naturally curled into apathetic smirks.

All of these things filter into our sense of security in our relationships. If everything around us is in decay, then why should love be any different? Why be faithful to a partner who doesn't satisfy us in bed when there's that person at work who can get the job done and knows how to keep his or her mouth shut? Hell, our coworkers will even watch the door so we don't get our pay docked. Why should we bind ourselves in holy matrimony when all the married people we see and know tied the knot only because they wanted to have that ceremony they always dreamed about?

I don't always live in this kind of paranoia, but many of my partners and homegirls do. Raised by single mothers, or the products of divorce, many are overwhelmed by the chiding of female elders who tell them the most important thing for them to do with their lives is to be a man's wife. This is to come before having a successful career, before having the best education, even before finding the kind of personal happiness that is key before you can become someone else's ideal partner.

These young women I speak of are of a type I cross paths with rather often, those who make checklists before they go out on dates and conference on what they'll say if he proposes, after date number three. They are my female friends who truly believe it's a reflection on them if things don't work out right away. Or if things are going too well, they push their Mr. Right away before he has a chance to give them the dream they've been waiting for. Plagued by sexual abuse, rape, and other untreated issues, they even find themselves fearing the men who love them most.

So many of us brothers suffer from different but equally virulent issues. Growing up too often without our fathers or other role models, we've come to define manhood as acts of violence on DVD, of preparing for a beef when someone bumps our shoulder, and smacking that ass in the backseat of a drop-top coup on the closest video channel. We accept the pimp as the ideal figure of strength and cunning. We fear that marriage is nothing but a trick for our women to get half of what little we own through divorce, and thus swear we'll never walk down the aisle.

This is not to say that these issues didn't exist for the generations that came before us. But these challenges have a different meaning in the face of a brave new world that is almost always in flux. Add in the fact that our community has yet to fully wield the spending power and political power we have to our advantage, and the future often looks bleak for our history makers of tomorrow. Our dreams of having the nice normal families that someone once told us America was all about aren't even substantive enough to fantasize about.

To make it worse, there are few people we're even willing to listen to, or who will listen to us. Our parents' leaders have become embarrassments, trapped in one scandal or the next. Or they dismiss the music and culture we so desperately cling to, our only blanket in an ice-cold generation gap.

Our parents failed us in trying to be different. Yes, they fought and died to attain far more freedom for us than they ever had. But their attempts to break away from the conflicted relationships of their own parents failed to provide us with the new familial foundations we needed.

I clearly remember moments when Mom and Dad were happy. I remember Angela and her bulb-shaped 'fro as my father held her tight in our kitchen, the two of them slow dancing to the music in their minds after a long day. I remember waking up in the middle of the night and being able to go into their room and lie down in the space between them until I went to sleep. I remember each of them taking one of my wrists and flinging me through the air until I squealed.

But I also remember that pair of pants being hurled at my head, and the fight in the foyer between them over the C I got on my sixth-grade report about Tunisia. I remember struggling to wake my mother in the mornings because the alarm never did the job, because she was often too sad to face the impending day. And I remember my father's journeys into the night after he put me to bed, his '87 Escort taking him toward taverns and secret rendezvous to ease the pain of starting all over again.

That was marriage to me, that kind of warmth and happiness, that kind of crippling defeat. When I was young I loved it so much that I wanted it right away, with every little grade-school girl I found to be the least bit cute: Takia Martin, Ebony Dempsey, and Kenisha Love. It pissed me off that I would have to wait another fifteen to twenty years before I could have that, before I could be that Mom and Dad kind of happy.

But later on when I came closer to finding that warmth with a woman, things got complicated. I had this need to prove that I could be better than any other man, that I could be strong enough for two, that I could fill all the gaps and make everything what it needed to be, so that neither of us would ever have to leave the other. I wanted to be a hero, Superman, everything Mom and Dad were not, just so that my future wouldn't end up like their past.

With these elements of my parents' relationship as my model, neither of my grandparents' marriages ever seemed to make much sense. I understood that they were older and far beyond the lovey-dovey newness that my parents were still embracing when I was a little kid. But the way I saw it, my grandparents could never be happy because they didn't seem like they were in love. And if they weren't in love, then how could it work?

I saw Jesse kiss Sally Helen only once or twice in twenty-seven years. They held hands about three times. He spoke to her only when he wanted to either eat or use her as a verbal target. And that was it. My dad's parents were a little better, but I could still see that they got on each other's nerves at least half the time.

Yet and still my grandparents stayed together until death parted them. They kept their vows. They remained in the same home and raised their children together. Their children married and gave them grandkids for them to shower with love whenever they visited. And I want that too.

If I can speak for my generation, I think that deep down we all want both. We all want to find someone whom we can love and trust, whom we can make love to for the rest of our lives and raise kids with. We wouldn't mind silver and gold anniversaries, and never to even think of leaving.

But how can we have something that we've so rarely seen? Many don't have the cerebral Polaroids I possess from my early years. We don't know what healthy relationships look like outside of sitcoms and what goes up on the big screen. How can we trust when we see our peers getting low-down and dirty on our daily installments of *Divorce Court* and *Jerry Springer*? There's no paradigm from which to create the marriages we want. And there's no clear idea on how to start assembling one.

There have been two or three times when I thought my number was up, when I rose with her in the morning and made coffee and breakfast before we showered together. Each time I could imagine doing this every day. I could imagine adding little ones to the mix. When a period was late, there was an unconscious prayer that this might be it, that the two of us would be responsible for making a life together.

Then weeks, or months, or years would pass and something would happen. She went to make peace with an ex-boyfriend only to fuck him. She swore all my female friends wanted to fuck me. She popped up with gonorrhea and I didn't, or threatened suicide, or drank herself into a stupor every other night so she could live with the fact that her father was a psychotic asshole.

They all came to me like moths to a flame, seeking love and attention, seeking my time, and furthermore seeking a way out of their own problems by trying to get me to solve them for them. They kept taking until there was nothing left, until I'd reduced myself to a low-budget Tony Robbins just to make it through a meal. Yet they always wondered what had happened to the old me, never realizing that it was they who had slowly filed me away.

I am at this bar on this night because I can't do it anymore, because all I've got is two empty clips and a sword worn dull. If reciprocity is pie in the sky, then I'll have to grow wings, because I'm tired of picking up other people's pieces.

According to my mother, true love shouldn't work this way. A true partner should always be there. According to my father, you can never anticipate what's going to happen in a relationship. All the both of you can do is try to see things in terms of what's really important.

If the Lone Ranger had his way, I should be the king of my castle. I should determine all of the variables and remain rigid while those around me do the bending.

I don't know who to listen to. And that is the problem.

provider

1

Love, compromise, and the cracking of the not-so-literal lash. These are the means by which a father maintains order, especially when he carries the only Y chromosome in his particular domicile. It is a cool Saturday in March of '04 and I stand in the foyer at the bottom of the stairwell, caught in the crossfire of desires between my two sisters and my stepmom, Carla, who has to hold down the fort while my dad and I are off on our designated mission. Imani, the younger, wants to go to the bookstore. Annia, the older (and ready to let everyone know it), wants to go to the movies. Carla wants to go to the bookstore too, which means that, by rule of majority, Annia will lose this round while I have a rare few hours to spend with my old man alone.

I pull a sharp U to head back out of his subdivision, a pretty place where the view of the heavens is as

The Jasper Family: Volume 2—(from left to right) my father, Annia, Imani, Carla, and their dog Diva

clear as Sally Helen's crystal. On the right night all you need is the naked eye to take in every star imaginable.

The current Jasper residence is less than twenty minutes from the bungalow where I grew from boy to man, the two-bedroom with a basement Pop snagged for us just before I started the eighth grade. He, like so many others, chose to abandon the city for Prince Georges County, the then up-and-coming suburb that would eventually grow into one of the most powerful enclaves of middle-class Black folks in the nation.

It is within that old bungalow that many of my memories of us as "best friends" reside. There was that infamous lecture when he implored my fifteen-year-old self to change my thought process. The words offered me were genius, or at least they seemed that way to an adolescent mind. I told him I wanted to know what was wrong with me because I couldn't get a girl to save my life.

"Instead of asking what's wrong with *you,* why don't you ask what's wrong with *them*?" he responded.

Part artist, part philosopher, part chef, do-it-yourselfer, and, of course, real estate appraiser, Melvin Nathaniel Jasper, Jr., always seemed to have the answers. He always knew what to say when I needed him to speak, the words destined to ease my mind like the Arrested Development track of the same name.

"You're my best buddy in the whole world," he'd say. My role as best man in his second wedding proved it.

I've traveled down from Brooklyn for this outing, for without it this section of the story cannot begin. I am working backward in time, moving up out of the various levels of the silent but still Dante-like hell created by the Lone Ranger's departure. And for this canto, Mel "Jazz" Jasper, Jr., will be my guide.

"What do you want to see?" he asks me as we approach Southern Avenue, the line that separates the County from Southeast DC, my *other* childhood home.

"I just wanna see your life," I say simply, though I know the request is far too broad, particularly when I know the exact slice of time I need him to revisit.

It's odd for both of us that I'm at the wheel, when for so long it's been the other way around. Pop has shuttled me across many state lines, to poetry readings and Tae Kwon Do exams, to toy stores and bookstores, formal dances, basement parties that pushed until three in the morning, and flights that took off long before sunrise. He has been there, in every way, because his father was just as present for him.

One of my last images of my father's father is of him sitting shotgun in a Ford Escort awfully similar to the Focus I'm currently whipping. Dying of stomach cancer, he wanted my dad and me to take him back to his old neighborhood, to the half of Georgetown that used to be all Black, its streets teeming with both working-class folks and those up to no good.

Mel, Sr., or "Buster," as he was affectionately known by both family and friends, was born on August 5, 1929, to William and Marian Jasper. Marian (or "Ma-Maran," as my father called her when he was too young to properly enunciate it), had come to DC from rural Virginia sometime in the 1920s. She met William shortly after and when the time came to tie the knot they made their first home in a small basement apartment supered by Will's father, William "Pa" Jasper, Sr., on G-town's Twenty-fourth Street, only a block or two away from the area that would one day become George Washington University, the institution of higher learning that would build the hospital where I would be born nearly fifty years later.

Will was a moody and verbally abusive man who showed his true colors later than sooner. A material provider for the kids in their early years, he offered less and less as time went on. "I think he hated Buster," Ma-Maran once told my father and me a few years before she passed away in '99 at the age of ninety-one. "That's probably the reason why I left him."

Growing up, Buster was a star athlete, having earned all-city titles in football, basketball, and baseball, yet he still made time to cook most meals for his younger siblings on the nights his mother worked. He did it all knowing that others needed him, that he was helping to keep it all going. He was always there for his family, until he turned nineteen, and ended up starting his own.

He married my paternal grandmother, Anne Shin, straight out of high school. My father was their firstborn barely a year later. Anne and Buster remained together until he passed on in February of '88.

It was Buster, my father's father, who picked me up from school on Thursday afternoons and drove me all the way uptown to WTTG-TV, where I served as one of four on-air kid personalities for a show called *Newsbag*. He'd have a story to tell me every trip, a new tale about his years in the Korean War, or about current events, or the Redskins, to whom he

was more devoted than any other fan. There was even a special whistle he'd use upon entering the gate surrounding the
family apartment just so I'd run to the door and open it,
knowing that it was him.

I'll never forget the Sunday mornings when Buster took
me to the open-air market on Florida Avenue to get the gro-
ceries for Sunday dinner. I was so small that he had to lift me
up to the counter so that I could get ahold of the blocks of
sharp Cheddar he'd always buy for me. Then we'd go home
and I'd help him tear the kale from the stems with *The
McLaughlin Group* or *CBS Sunday Morning* playing in the
background. He was like a second father.

I can still hear his weak murmur of a voice as we drove
him through his old stomping grounds that one last time. The
apartment building where he had lived was an empty lot
framed by the concrete masonry that had been there since he
was a little boy. Blackie's, one of the premier restaurants in that
colored part of town, was still in business. He rattled off stories like rounds from an endless arsenal, the brim of his fish-
erman's cap pulled low as he slunk into the reclined seat, his
once husky frame having grown frail after the chemo and ra-
diation therapy.

He was giving us all that he had left, all he could offer up
before the lights went out. I think he knew that he wasn't going to make it, that the daily doses of Marlboros and Teacher's
had finally taken their toll. Or had it been the stress of a complicated marriage and the trials he'd endured as a provider that
had earned him an early passage to the other side at the age
of fifty-seven?

I dreamt about Buster's death the night before it happened. There was the image of a police car parked in front of
the three-story where he'd spent his last years. I saw my father

coming down the basement stairs no sooner than I was through the door, and he was telling me that my second father was gone. And that was just how it happened. I turned onto Adrian Street from Texas Avenue and the cop car was sitting there. When I came through the door my father was descending the stairwell to hit me with the news. My subconscious had seen the future. Yet I never said a word about it.

I remember walking to the back of the house and climbing our slope of a yard to the redwood chairs there and crying until my eyes hurt. It was the greatest loss I'd felt at twelve, and in some ways still is.

I didn't have the same sense of loss about the Lone Ranger. His world as I knew it was devoid of color and warmth. His was a life spent between the shadows of his room and the same daily routine. Get up. Go to work. Come home. Eat. Sleep. Then do it all over again.

There were so few smiles, so few hands-on lessons from grandfather to grandson. Losing him was like losing a stranger in some ways, yet in others it was like losing all I knew. I loved Buster for what he did and said, for giving me a million reasons to smile and grow and have a good time. Jesse Langley's power came from being the only two things he knew how to be: a father and provider. It was his seed that created his children, and his toil that sustained them until they could do it on their own. Plain and simple, the only way a Greenville boy like him would've had it.

My grandfathers met only once in their lifetimes, even though they lived within blocks of each other for more than a decade. And that was at my parents' wedding. They shared so much yet nothing at all, the paradox that is being part of an extended family.

Back in the present, Pop and I pass the Congressional Cemetery on D Street where John Philip Sousa and other local history makers rest in peace. Then comes the DC jail, where we've both visited friends, then the armory, home to the Ringling Brothers Circus that Buster made sure I saw almost every year of my childhood. It's also where Dad learned to fire a gun under the same man's tutelage.

I make a left on Holbrook Street—I know this neighborhood like the back of my hand. It would not be itself without the barking of dogs, or the omnipresent sound of balls bouncing out-of-bounds, or the yelling of boy-men during hours when everything should be calm and quiet. I have laid there, played there, and set off a few grand's worth (literally) of illegal fireworks into its skies on various Fourths of July. But while I know it, my father has lived it.

We turn onto Childress from Holbrook and cruise past the Langley residence, both of us giving it a proper nod of recognition. Then it's a right on Trinidad Avenue followed by another left onto Mount Olivet Road. We pass the newly renovated Bethesda Baptist Church, "the scene of the crime," as my dad puts it, referencing its significance as the place where my parents were married.

We almost head down a one-way street until I see the DO NOT ENTER sign and make a quick 180 Bat-turn. Pop explains that the street used to go both ways. Some things have changed.

But the change hasn't been for the better in these blocks known as Ivy City. Where there was once green grass there is now barren soil. Where there was once business, there is now an excess of decaying space for rent. My father vaguely recognizes the faces of two men talking on a corner, but he tells me to keep moving.

What's left of Crummell Elementary School, the school my parents attended together, is surrounded by a rusting chain-link fence topped with razor wire. The building's brick walls are enveloped by dried vines and dead leaves. Only splinters of glass remain in the window frames, and you can barely make out the chiseled letters on the front entrance. The school is an easy walk down from Trinidad, long enough to enjoy the sun in summer and quick enough to beat the cold when temperatures drop.

"See that white building over there?" my dad says, pointing a few blocks down. "That used to be a coffee shop that this Greek guy owned." He spends a minute or two searching his mental Rolodex for the man's name. But in the end it escapes him.

"And as you see, it's right across from the main building for Hecht's," he continues. "That's where my father worked for a long time, driving for them. He had that job before he went to the war, and they kept it for him until he came back.

"So he'd eat there at the coffee shop on his lunch break. And when he was done he'd come over to the playground at the school and I'd get to see him. I pretty much saw him every day. Most of the guys I knew didn't have that." They didn't see their fathers at all.

There's only a single letter of difference in the name of Kovak's Liquor store, a place now teeming with activity in the late afternoon, when compared to what it was in my father's day.

"It used to be Kojak's," Pop informs me as he unzips his coat. The heat in my little Ford rental is too much for both of us. I am part of the legacy of "The Polar Bears," as my mother called my father and grandfather, because for some reason it takes a lot for us to get cold.

"At first it was only a liquor store, but later they opened

up the carry-out next to it. And me and my boys used to get pocket money when the Kojak brothers needed people to circulate flyers around the area. We'd put them on posts and on doorsteps and in all the apartment buildings we could. And they gave us a buck for that, one buck for all of us."

We finally arrive at 1243 Simms Place, the two-story complex Buster, Anne, and their two young sons called home. For a time Annette, my great-aunt, and her husband, my uncle Joe, lived in the building just across the alley. And my aunt Alice, Ma-Maran's sister, and her husband, Lloyd, lived two buildings back. There was family all around, all of them young couples just starting out.

The rent was affordable. The streets were clean, and young Melvin had a wondrous labyrinth in which to come of age. He did well in his studies, but his real school was the neighborhood itself, one great wide stretch for a young and curious mind to explore. He looks up at the building as if he just moved out yesterday.

"The people across the hall were the shouting Pentecostal holiness people whose son would get so drunk that he'd pass out in the basement. People would go down to dump the trash and see his feet sticking out and think it was a dead body. Your grandfather would go down there and be like 'Junior, get up! You're scarin' the hell out of these people!'

"Below us was the Haitian lady, Ms. Edith. And she'd be doing all of her voodoo stuff, which scared the hell out of my mother. I remember there was one time when my little brother Mike would always jump down steps, from one landing to the next. And it'd make a lot of noise. One day Ms. Edith came out and caught him and threatened to cut his legs off if he made that much noise again. I don't know why she went and said that."

Mike told his father, and that was not a good thing for Ms. Edith.

"Pop went down there to say something to her and her boyfriend was coming out of the apartment and looked up at him. Pop said, 'What the fuck you want!' And the man ran back into the apartment and then Ms. Edith came out. Pop told her, 'Don't ever threaten my children again! Cuz I'll kill you and your boyfriend!'

"After that we didn't have any more problems with them. Pop was a big guy. A very gentle man, but he didn't stand for anyone messin' with the family."

It's a treat and a half to be rolling with my dad like this, just the two of us. It's just like it was my first seventeen years, he and I on the move together, best friends exploring the world together. For any question I had, he had an answer. For any problem, he had a solution. When no one else seemed to understand me or what I needed, the right words were always on the tip of his tongue. I'm proud to hear from my two beautiful little sisters that he's exactly the same thing for them.

We make more turns through blind alleys and obscure passageways. He shows me places sectioned off by countless steel fences that used to be open areas. I see what's left of the blacktop where stickball games were played. The grass was as green as the pimped-out DeVille we pass in one of the driveways, its stacked headlights polished to a gleaming shine.

He points out the remains of the tall brick wall all the boys used to jump off. Now an arthritic, the very thought of it makes his knees hurt. He also tells me about the construction crawl spaces in the basements of some of the apartment buildings and how all the kids would use them to move from one building to the next. "If our parents knew we were doing it,

Dad and I at the Million Man March in 1995.

they would have been mortified," he says with a grin. "But this was our little world."

From there it's on to the rear quarter of Gallaudet University, the nation's first college for the deaf. The school was smaller in my father's youth. Most of the land was just woods where Pop and the boys took refuge in the summer after stealing watermelons from the cart man on Florida Avenue. Sometimes they'd even make it out with the slippery fruit intact. "But half the time somebody would drop it."

Trinidad Avenue and its surrounding blocks weren't just a neighborhood. They were a community, a place where everyone was trying to get by, a place where folks had lived worse and were not hoping for something better, together.

"Everybody knew everybody. And in the summers no one had central air. At that time there weren't even window air-conditioners to be purchased. Those little apartments got hot as all get-out. So on summer nights everyone would come out and sit on the stoops and have all of their windows open. There was a kind of rhythm to the place.

"The Colemans lived on the corner," he says, pointing from the front of his old building. "There were the Browns, the Bankses, the Butlers, and the Palimore brothers. One of them is a street musician downtown I used to see a lot. The Deloach family lived next door, and Mr. Deloach and my father had known each other as boys.

"And there were two stores on opposite ends of the street, both owned by Jews. One was owned by a couple. The old man, Mr. Ben, had a palsy of some kind and spoke with slurred speech. So his wife really ran the place. They were nice folks. The other one was run by these two nasty brothers. We never went down there, but some people did. My boy Hawk's mother would go down there and curse them out on a regular basis."

A loose Doberman charges into the alley where we're parked as if it's being chased. I haven't seen that breed for years since it lost the dog popularity contest to the pit bull as the inner-city hound of choice.

"Get us out of here," Pop says blankly as the dog rushes past the passenger side. I gladly oblige him.

We end up in the alley that separates Mount Olivet Road from Childress Street. To the left are passing cars and to the right is the Lone Ranger's domain. My father looks straight ahead, past the basketball courts and playground to the wide field where Ruth K. Webb Elementary School, the school he and my mother attended after Crummell, now sits.

"We used to call this Florence Hill," he says, "because when we were kids there was an Asian girl named Florence Lee who got sexually assaulted there. And you know how kids are. The names stick. Later on they cut some of the top off of it to build the playground and the rec center, but it was really good for sledding when it snowed. We'd ride our bikes around it and it was where the neighborhood football team, the Rockets, used to come and practice."

He tells me about a battle that took place on the very spot where we're parked. The guys from his block came across some poor dude who didn't know well enough not to be walking through their side of Trinidad. And in the timeless tradition of neighborhood turf marking, the boys gave him a thorough jumping in the alleyway and left him to lick his wounds. But ten minutes later, to their surprise, the kid was back with nine other boys. Pop and his previously cohesive crew scattered like rats, some to take beatings while others made cowardly exits. "Friendships broke up over that shit," he laughs.

"It was a tough place, but it wasn't like now when everyone can get hold of a firearm," he observes. "You had to be able to rumble. As a matter of fact, one of the ways that you gained initiation into a gang back then was by fighting one of the gang members. That was the way it was determined where you stood in terms of ranking with everybody else." Occasionally a blade was pulled, but no one got aired out with the closest pistol. That's my generation's way of doing things.

By the time Dad was enrolled in Eastern High School, things weren't so picturesque on Trinidad's blocks. The mid-'60s and '70s marked one of the first major floods of heroin into Black communities nationwide. And many of the young men my dad knew took hits. Danny, a kid from a better-off family at the top of Childress, died of an overdose. And he was not the last. My uncles Mike and Gary would both be tested by the lethal currents of addiction. The Jaspers moved out of Trinidad in 1966 to their first home in Benning Heights when my Dad was seventeen.

The empty lot between Kovak's and a convenience store that used to be a 7-Eleven is overrun with addicts. I know they use by the way they move, that intoxicated swagger, or the cranial drift that often accompanies the "nod." One of them, a caramel-colored bag of bones who was once someone's queen, yells something after us, maybe because we locked eyes, or more likely because she has no one familiar left to speak to.

"I had to stop coming around here," Pop says, looking away from the scene as the woman fades from the rearview. "It's just too painful."

On the way out we stop to idle in front of the Lone Ranger's house one more time. My father can remember when the front door was different and when different cars were parked in the head of household's designated space.

"He'd always be out there, sitting on the porch smoking," he remembers. "That's where he'd be." We go south to Holbrook and hang a left. It's time for him to return home.

2

When I was a little boy, I would get down on my knees at night with hands clasped, my mother right beside me. We would ask God to bless all the people we knew. And since I knew only a handful, my mother would feed me names. After my grandparents and uncles, my teacher and my neighbors, came my two aunts: Jackie and Loretta, two of the best friends my mother has ever had, and two women I have never really gotten to know beyond cheek kisses and respectful hellos over the phone. Aunt Loretta had a daughter named Rashida, and from time to time we'd all go out, and "Shida Bug" and I would play together. Our mothers would always remind us that we were due on the same day. I arrived early on November 20. Rashida came late on December 4. Shida and I were night and day, a fact that proved to be most embarrassing during a certain plane flight to Orlando, Florida, during which Shida loudly screamed and complained for most of the two-hour flight because I had the window seat, and, while attempting to sleep, I had decided to keep the shade closed.

My aunt Jackie, however, had been far more distant. For me, she was mostly an image behind the transparent sheets of old scrapbooks, or a topic of discussion between my mother and grandmother on the Sundays we visited Childress Street. My little mind figured out that Jackie now lived somewhere else, because it was a big deal whenever she came to visit. At the time she then lived nearly four hours away, in a place I'd later know as Brooklyn, New York.

Jackie Johnson knew the neighborhood even before my parents did. A year ahead of both at Crummell, she was the very first Black child to live on Holbrook Street, between Levis and Mount Olivet Road. It was 1952 and the more residential side of the neighborhood was still mostly white, which made her the fly in the buttermilk, though she would never have understood the phrase at the time.

She and her parents were the first African Americans to move into the complex at 1655 Holbrook when she was five. At the time, the Langleys were still living on New York Avenue. They would not get to Childress Street for almost another two years.

"My father was light enough to pass," she recalls in a telephone conversation on a warm August evening. "So when he went to get the apartment, they thought he was white. But after we moved in the neighbors started complaining because of the brown wife and brown daughter. It became a big mess. The man who owned our building owned a lot of houses in Trinidad, but he never put us out. He even worked out an agreement with my father, because my father was a carpenter. So Daddy ended up taking care of the carpentry maintenance for the exterior of the building."

Young Jacqueline was living proof that racism is not inherent but taught. Like most children of color she had no idea what her difference in shade would mean.

"There was a white girl around my age who lived in the apartment building on the corner. I remember I was playing with her in her hallway and her mother came out and saw the two of us playing and immediately called her in. As the girl was walking up the steps, I heard the mother tell her 'I told you not to play with any niggers!' "

Jackie didn't know what the word *nigger* meant. So she went home and told her mother what had happened. She remembers seeing her mother's face drop. She had never discussed such things with her only child.

"When my father came home he tried to explain it to me," Jackie continues, "but of course I didn't understand it because nobody had prepared me for that kind of a thing."

There was a chubby little white boy who lived in the apartment building at the bottom of Childress, a building that had a swing in front that all of the kids used to play on. Jackie was over there playing with him one day and it was her turn to get on when another white boy told her, "No niggers can get on the swing."

The chubby boy stepped in front of his friend and said, "If she can't swing, then I won't swing either." The boy then grabbed Jackie by the hand and dragged her up the street and away from the young bigot in training. Yet she still didn't understand all of that "nigger" stuff. She would figure it out, though, in the years to come, as the '50s became the '60s.

"When I think of Trinidad, the first thing that comes to my mind is this poem by Nikki Giovanni, "Nikki-Rosa," something about being raised in the ghetto and that she didn't realize that she came from a ghetto until she became an adult. We were living in what was considered one of the roughest sections of the city. But it was a community.

"Everyone helped raise each other's children. And as kids we were very happy. We didn't realize that we were poor. We did a lot of things that kids are bound to do. Making excursions here and there. We were really involved with the rec center across the street from Angela's house, because it was like the center of the community.

"In the summer and on the weekends we'd get up in the morning, head to the rec, and stay there all day. We'd take little breaks to go home and have lunch, but then we'd be right back up there. That was back when the city was very involved in providing services for children."

I can see it. Cheerleading and football. Jacks, marbles, and double Dutch. The junior Rockets throwing balls back and forth on Florence Hill with the sun beaming overhead. Trinidad was a place of hope for those young parents, a piece of a dream miles from what its Black residents had known before. And the Lone Ranger would be in his chair on the porch, right across the street from the playground, taking it all in.

"Mr. Langley was always on that front porch. The man worked, but he was always on the front porch. If he wasn't sitting on that porch he was just getting out of his car coming home. On the outside he was always stern, but deep down you knew he was a pussycat. I really realized how much of a pussycat he was when Melvin and Angela were getting married."

It was a night a few months before the wedding and Jackie was coming home from night school. Since she had a few dollars in her pocket, she decided to hail a cab. That cab just happened to be Jesse's.

"He was so excited about the two of them getting married, and he talked and talked and talked about what a nice couple they were. But just the next day I saw him on the porch back in the neighborhood. Your father walked up and Mr. Langley gave him this really stern 'hello,' and then just walked away from him. Whenever he'd see Melvin he'd kind of growl at him."

The tale forces my lips to curl, because it gives me the perfect explanation for a relationship that never made sense to me. Melvin and Jesse were never too big on small talk. There was respect, but my father, even as a teenager, didn't like the way his future father-in-law ran his household.

Unlike Mel, Sr., Jesse played the "king of the castle" role to the hilt. When you came through the door it was your duty to pay tribute, to speak only when spoken to, to dodge whatever he threw your way. And he was always so hard on his children, particularly Gary. Kissing the ring had never been a requirement in young Melvin's house. And he wasn't going to do it in anyone else's.

I think of one story that illustrates their tension best. It was

November 22, 1975, and I had barely been in the world for forty-eight hours. All was quiet in my father's house. My mother was in bed recovering from labor, and young Melvin was lying next to her trying to catch up on some much-needed shut-eye when something pulled my father awake.

Someone was opening the front gate. A moment later there was a pounding on the front door. Groggy and somewhat irritated, he went to the door to find Jesse, accompanied by some relative my father had never seen before, yelling repeatedly, "Let me get in there and see my grandbaby!"

There had been no call in advance or any consideration for my mother's need for rest. It was all about what Jesse wanted. And Pop wasn't having it.

He opened the door but blocked Jesse and this other relative from coming in. Voices were raised. For once in his life, the Old Man was going to have to abide by someone else's rules.

Dad refused to let them in, denying Jesse the visit he believed to be his right. The older man went home in disgust. The younger man went back to tend to his family, hoping he wouldn't have to go through anything like that again. And he didn't. It was probably the first time anyone in Jesse's immediate circle had stood up to him. After that, you couldn't get more than a "hello" and "good-bye" between them, all the way until the end.

Once, however, maybe a year or two before he passed on, the Lone Ranger and I were seated on the infamous porch at the end of a spring. Out of the blue he asked me how Melvin was and what he was up to. I told him about my dad's real estate appraising and his two new daughters. Then I mentioned the area where he lived, and Jesse guesstimated his location down to the exact road that led to his place of residence.

"I always respected him," he told me, as if revealing one of his deepest secrets. "I never had anything against him."

But returning to the golden age of Trinidad, Jackie informs me that the Langley home was "the place" on Childress Street.

"Angela didn't have to be home. If you knew the Langleys, you just ran through the house. The door was always open to all the kids in the neighborhood. You sat down at the table and you got ready to eat. You didn't even think about it."

Sally Helen always cooked for more than she was expecting. Jackie, as an only child, went there as often as she could, finding that "something that was missing in her own house." There she was one of the family, playing in the front and backyards like she was Sally Helen's own daughter.

Loretta Sanford found herself at the Langley home searching for the same missing ingredient in her family life. She was raised by her mother and grandparents between two apartments on 1230 Bladensburg Road, and her parents never lived in the same space. Thus her father was little more than a voice on the other end of a phone line.

Mr. Langley was the closest thing to a father she ever had. He was kind and loving and always there to protect her, to make sure that things were going alright. For her, going to see Angela was like going home. And home was where she loved to be.

Girls like Loretta were far from atypical in the neighborhood. Even then single-parent homes were the norm in certain sections of town. The causes, of course, were all too familiar: death, divorce, abandonment, and fathers who dodged the opportunity to help harvest what they'd sown.

The difference was that back then there were far more surrogates willing to step in and fill the gaps, men like the Lone Ranger, who welcomed all in exchange for a certain kind of respect, a kind of allegiance to his way of life that most of the kids were willing to pledge.

Jackie was one of the fortunate ones. Her father, a mechanic and carpenter, made Saturdays their days on the town. Though he wasn't an educated man, he took her to museums and art galleries, trips that served as the first exposure to cultures other than her own. She watched him work and asked him questions about everything she could. Unfortunately, he later became an alcoholic and their relationship became strained. Fortunately, they were able to reconcile before his death in 1999 due to a liver-related illness.

Having a relationship with her father gave her a sense of strength, a kind of security. Though she knows she'll hear about it for airing Loretta's dirty laundry, she remembers a time in the girls' teens when her fatherless friend started dating a man who was old enough to be her daddy. The fling didn't last long, partially because Jackie and my mother weren't big fans of it. To this day Jackie thinks Loretta did it because she was searching for that paternal energy she'd lacked in her day-to-day beyond what her grandfather could offer.

I think of all the young black girls who never had a man to call Daddy, who learned what they know of men on the screens large and small and in the faces of the boys who hollered at them from the corner because of their sprouting chests or the size of their behinds. They didn't grow up with a man telling them they're beautiful, or intelligent, or even capable of living a life outside of the blocks they called home. I wonder how different their worlds would be if they had.

"Angela said something to me back when I was in my twenties," Jackie reveals. "We were talking about our fathers and I remember she told me that while we may have had problems with our fathers, that they may have created issues in our homes, the fact was that they were present and we didn't hunger for a father like most of the kids around us."

Like most childhood friends, the trio started coming apart as high school came to a close. Jackie, the eldest and a year ahead in school, started to hang with a girl named Diana, who was in her year and had moved in next door to her. Jackie started pulling away, not just from her girls, but from the neighborhood itself.

"The neighborhood made a change for the worse as I got older. When I was younger I didn't see the poverty, but as the old people moved out and different people moved in we started seeing more violence. Gangs started developing. Friends we'd grown up with got on drugs and got killed. And it seemed like it all happened overnight."

She wanted to be an actress and a model. But most of all she just wanted to get away from home and out of DC. She didn't like the cliquishness about the city, or the class hierarchy. In DC, someone might make a point of saying they had met a GS-14 (a higher government employment class ranking) instead of a person who happened to work for the government. Or a coworker might ask you why you're hanging out with the secretary at lunch when you've got a college degree.

She couldn't stand that kind of thing. She had to get away.

By thirty, she was living in Brooklyn. She liked the fact that there were so many kinds of people to meet, so many experiences without the constraints that DC culture had placed on her. She never ran out of things to see or do and every day was different. These things sound so familiar to me, because they were my reasons for fleeing the area at seventeen, when a set of scholarships and a slot on the roster at Morehouse gave me a free ride out of town.

But for all three friends things turned out frighteningly similarly. They all divorced but excelled in the lives they lived. Retirement is now within all of their grasps. Jackie, the student of cultures, can tell you of the countless phenomena occurring on the planet at any given moment.

Loretta, who has worked for the U.S. Department of Transportation since high school, was recently one of the first Black women to be appointed to the new Transportation Security Administration. These days she also boasts of a thirty-year-old daughter with two degrees who's preparing to pursue a third.

My mother's at the top of her game in the education racket with a kid who gets paid to do what he would've always done for free.

They're a long way from the days of the rec center, though the building still stands as it has for more than forty years. Jackie has returned to DC and the three have fallen back into their own rhythm. I saw them reunited for the first time at a barbecue celebration for the publication of my first novel. The synergy between them hasn't changed one bit in almost fifty years. They are a triple setting of gems mined and manicured in the streets of Trinidad, and still sparkling for all the world to see.

As I cradle the receiver, a literal tingle descends my spine. Now I feel like I'm starting to get somewhere. My dear aunt Jackie has just told me about two different men, one of them the iron-handed recluse I felt I knew too well. The other is the "pussycat" hidden within the clothes of a stern provider, a stoic working man who wanted only the best for his first and only daughter, someone who could express his joy to anyone outside the house where he had to run things.

They are two men who inhabited the same frame, but did they live there at the same time? Did something happen that turned the latter into the former? Was there a final straw that broke that pussycat's back? This is what I'm searching for, and what I hope to find as my journey takes me back into the Langley home, up the stairs and to the left, to the son who knew his father best.

3

To quote the words of one of our current pseudo-academic, rhyming jackleg preacher-leaders, drugs have always been the easiest means of subjugating a people. One need only look to the lotus eaters in Homer's *Odyssey*, or to the opium addiction that sealed the Chinese within their own trade. Or you can just look out on the block at the women and men you know, or used to know, before they were taken under by whichever high was the rage when they first got hooked.

I was still in the single digits when me and my main man James "Butchie" Cunningham wandered the hills and dales of Fairfax Village, a then havenlike set of town houses and apartment buildings on the edge of Southeast DC. We were playing by one of the trash dumpsters we found so much joy in climbing into every once in a while, or maybe we were near one of the muddy patches where the inclined streets happened to erode the greenery. That was where you were most likely to find the needles.

We knew what that first one was when we saw it. We'd been to the doctor to get our shots. We'd watched *Knight Rider* or *The A-Team* or any other show where the truth serum was injected via syringe. Someone had thrown this one away because they didn't need it anymore. So it was ours to do with as we wished.

We filled it with rainwater and squirted the thin stream against the ground, then at each other. Somewhere along the way the syringe managed to break from one drop to the ground too many. Looking back, it was only the grace of God that kept us safe.

We figured out the danger in the years ahead, when Nancy Reagan's "Just Say No" campaign would beat the antidrug dogma into our still-widening skulls. Shelly Yarborough, my fourth-grade classmate, got to visit good ole Nancy and the Gipper at the White House because she founded DC's first "Just Say No" club. Her mother once bragged to my own that they'd just come back from playing tennis with the Reagans. Even back then I wasn't impressed.

Yet when it came to my own neighborhood, saying no was far from enough. People I knew materialized on designated corners, dressed in designer track suits they shouldn't have been able to afford. They clipped pagers to their belts to accompany the knives and pistols they kept concealed in their waistbands. I still remember when one of them, a kid I went to school with, handed me fifty bags of crack rocks stapled together and asked me to run them down the street for him while I was walking my dog, Joe (RIP).

There was a moment of deliberation. I knew that there would be money at the end of the journey, money that might allow me to buy some fresher gear: a pair of Used Jeans or a Gore-Tex coat like the one my schoolmate was encased in.

Still, my head told me it was wrong. Taking that walk was a journey down a path I couldn't come back from. So I dropped the bag in the hood of his fancy-ass coat, said a "Nah," and picked up the pace.

The last thing I remember was his conceited grin, as if to say that I'd be back, that I didn't have a choice. He was wrong about me, though I can't say the same for others in my circle of familiars.

I never saw that particular "hustla" again, though sometime just past my thirteenth birthday I did see the open apartment window two stories up. I was waiting for my uncle to appear there on that less than rosy strip of Texas Avenue, no more than a twenty-minute walk from the house Buster Jasper had bought to keep his kids away from the powder circulating in the streets of Trinidad. My grandfather had now been dead for the better part of six months, and his youngest son (left unnamed to protect his privacy) had taken the car a day and a half before and had not returned with it.

My father was around the front of the building, ringing the bell at the designated address before which the Lincoln Grand Marquis we sought was parked. We just needed to get the keys, so that we would get the car back to Buster's widow, our commander-in-chief on this particular exercise. I was at the rear of the building yelling my uncle's name loud enough to wake the dead—positioned throughout the apartment complex, those who regularly pushed down plungers or "beamed up Scottie" at the expense of everything they owned and held dear.

Five boys who looked about fourteen saw me standing there, alone, on a block that was not mine. I was not a critically acclaimed pugilist. I was not armed with an applicable weapon. And as those who know me best will tell you, my right leg has a tendency to tremble when I get really nervous. None of these were good things at the moment.

If they rushed me I would do my best to tag the leader, just once, right on the bridge of the nose or across the lower lip, something to make him bleed, something for him to remember me by when the day was over, or maybe even for a few more days to follow. All of this because my uncle had been pulled under by drugs.

It was one of those moments some might say defines your boyhood. My heart raced. My coordination went to mush. I just stood there frozen as the enemy approached. But just as they were upon me (meaning about twenty feet away), my uncle appeared from an open window above and told me that he was coming down. My would-be foes took his words as a confirmation that I had legit business on their turf and thus started back toward the direction from which they came. Moments away from taking a beatdown over something I shouldn't have had to deal with in the first place, I was living proof that addiction doesn't affect only the addict but everyone around him.

The years went by like seconds, with no way to turn back the clock. My uncle lost so much more before he finally broke free a decade-plus later, at forty-one. His hoop dreams, dreams that began with a basketball scholarship to the University of Maryland, ended up raisins in the sun. He ducked a hit-and-run charge by repeated trips to detox. He is now engaged and trying to make the best of life and the many years he has left. But I have another uncle who has yet to pry himself free of that same addiction's grip, a choke hold that his family is now enduring in the same way.

———

Gary Langley was living only a few blocks away when my younger uncle was making enemies jumping down stairwells on Simms Place. The third child of Sally Helen and the Lone Ranger, Gary is perhaps the best blend of his parents' genes. He wears his father's face and the lanky signature height of most of the Langley men I've known. But he's slender and toned like the Smiths of Powhatan, and has inherited their comedic disposition, always knowing how to move his people to laughter.

At his best Gary can do anything with his hands, from painting and plastering to changing oil and brake pads on your ride, from laying down wall-to-wall carpeting to wood finishing. I remember when I was seven cheering him on when he received his GED at thirty. I was proud that my un-

A twenty-something Gary on the sacred green
Langley couch. Note the plastic cover.

cle was doing his thing, and that he too was going to have his own job and home like the rest of the family. At least that was what I thought was going to happen.

Instead it was as if time stood still for more years than I could count. As his sister grayed and his little brother went bald, as my cousin Jay grew from an embryo to a star athlete, Gary remained trapped in the same place and time.

He still slept in the room next to his father's. He still came home in time for whatever meal his mother might be cooking. Jobs came and went. He came and went under shadow of night and borrowed things not likely to be returned.

I saw the future in these things because of that unnamed uncle, because of being there for his induction into the heroin hall of fame. And from all I could see, Gary's name would soon be added to the books, if it hadn't already. There were only three ways for it to end. One was for him to stop. Another was jail. The third was in a casket.

"I never want to say that I wish I had the chance to sit and do this with you," Gary began. " 'Cause like I say, I'm part of your frame of reference. Some of the things I say and do you'll benefit from, just from your being around me."

It's the Fourth of July 2003. The Fourth is a great day of Langley celebration beaten out only by Thanksgiving and Jesus' birthday. An iced cooler is filled to the brim with Pepsi, lemonade, and fruit punch. There's a pan full of grilled burgers and hot dogs next to the potato salad and cole slaw. There are also two bushels of steamed crabs, and four steamed lobsters, a rather surprising addition from my favorite uncle and the baby of the family, Anthony Caesar Langley.

The Langley house is still a place where folks from the neighborhood stop through from time to time. Lucille Jones, who grew up in the house next door, takes a seat on the green velvet chair, unaware that she will be one of its last occupants before it is replaced as a part of Sally Helen's renovations. My cousin Jay, first child of Jesse James Langley, Jr., the Lone Ranger's second child, sits on the couch, laughing as my mother, Tony, and Tony's best friend, Jerome, do covers of the songs they pull from the stack of 45s by the old phonograph. This decision to take it old school came after they all stumbled through the lyrics of a rather lackluster rendition of Nelly's "Hot in Here," which had thumped through the open doorway via one of the many booming systems cruising.

The trio jumps between decades and genres, from the Supremes (a song I don't quite know) to go-go godfather Chuck Brown's "Bustin' Loose" to Fats Domino's "Blueberry Hill." Sally Helen is laughing so hard that her eyes are shut.

It's the talent show that never ends, three middle-aged people recapturing moments in time that now exist only in memory and Time-Life throwback music collections. They help me to imagine the days Aunt Jackie spoke of, when this house was a place of love and good times for anyone who came through its doors. Yet and still it's not the same. We all feel the absence in this first year without him. We just don't talk about it.

"He made everybody's day," Gary says, leaning back against the couch on the enclosed rear porch, a paper plate of gutted crab shells before him. "He made sure that everything and everybody was alright. That's what I miss. You had to be alright around here. If you weren't, he was going to make sure that you were trying to get there."

Fashionwise, Gary's the guy who can get away with anything. I've seen him in light-colored slacks with fake alligator shoes and a skipper's hat, merlot-colored three-piece suits with matching brims and more Kangols and pleather coats than I'm sure even he can count. Like his father before him, he usually comes in the front door, says hello, and heads right upstairs to the little black-and-white TV and boom box in his room. And there he usually remains until it's time for a meal, a bootleg movie on the DVD player downstairs, or another journey out into the streets where he's dwelled for more than fifty-two years.

Gary's first memory of his father is also of the man sitting on that porch seat we keep hearing about.

"He was checkin' out everything. Observing. But he was never just looking at what was in front of him. He had eyes in the back of his head. He'd know about everything going on on that playground and in this house at the same time."

It is true that there was nothing that escaped the man's gaze. He could tell you the balances on all the monthly bills three months ahead, the average cost of an oversized grocery run for Turkey Day, and whether or not you'd washed your hands before dinner, all without giving you the impression that he knew anything about the three. His presence gave off a sense of perpetual ability, that he could handle whatever you threw his way. But he wanted you to throw only when you absolutely needed him.

For example, he dropped my mother little hints over the years about taking care of her car, little things he'd say or made sure that she saw him do, that would let her know how important auto maintenance was. After all, this was a man who changed his oil and brake pads himself and kept fan belts, fluid, and a garage worth of tools in his trunk. He was from a time when all service stations were closed to people with his shade of skin. When traveling he always avoided the interstate for Route 1 and stayed in the right lane, doing everything possible to avoid any road mishaps. I guess the proof is in the pudding because I've never heard of him having an accident or a problem with the law.

"He ain't never tell me nothin'," Gary says, corroborating my theory. "He showed me."

The Lone Ranger tried to show my mom on the car thing, though it didn't pan out the way either of them would have hoped. The engine in her Corsica locked on a muggy evening in July of 1995, right in front of the West gate of the U.S. Capitol, when I happened to be driving. Even though it was long before 9/11, my first love and I drew the attention of about six white Capitol cops. The tow truck couldn't get there fast enough. And when we finally did get the car home and its future looked bleak, it was the Lone Ranger who went out and found a new engine for it, then paid to have it installed out of his own pocket. The whole thing could have been avoided had Mom heeded his advice. Still it was a father's job to provide, so he did so, once again proving how much he loved his papoose.

But my mother was not the closest to him. Gary was. If Jesse was going anywhere, it was his third child who would be in the seat next to him.

"He was like my ace boon coon for real. I had other friends but that was my main man, and a father at the same time. Because I was more of a hardhead, just like him."

Maybe that accounts for the things young Melvin witnessed growing up, for the way Jesse was always hardest on his closest son. Even I can remember a few occasions when the Old Man was more than outspoken about his dislike of Gary's choices. He spoke out against Thelma, Gary's most recent significant other, the one who was ironically most concerned with helping the man she loved escape his addiction.

We were all seated at the table, less than ten minutes into

one Thanksgiving meal, when the Lone Ranger came down
to join us. The only words uttered that deep into grub time
were requests for various plates and bowls. But then my
grandfather took a seat as his wife made him a place. He was
silent, obviously distracted by something, his eyes avoiding
contact with the side of the table to his left where both Gary
and Thelma were seated. The rest of us thought nothing of it
as we enjoyed our meal and the company of our loved ones.
The Lone Ranger, however, had something on his mind.

He'd barely taken in a forkful when the patriarch glanced
at Thelma and then murmured a sentence that launched the
word *slut* in her direction. No one said anything. Not my
mother, not Sally Helen, not Thelma. It was Tony who
brought thunder down upon the table.

"Look, either you're gonna sit up here and behave or you
can go back upstairs with that foolishness!" he shouted. The
old man stopped where he was, avoiding Tony's gaze. A moment later he rose from the table and returned to his cham-
ber, not to be seen again. Up until that point I'd never seen
Tony yell at someone like that. He was apparently all too familiar with his father's darker behaviors.

I could only gather that Tony had had enough, that he'd
become sickened by such outbursts from his father. And then
and there, as a grown man who truly loved his mother and
siblings, he refused to take it anymore. Gary, however, just sat
there, defending neither himself nor his woman. Jesse Langley
was not a man he would make a foe of, especially not as long
as he was still living in his father's house.

"He was a real manipulator," Gary further explains about
his father. "He always wanted to be in charge and have his
way. He'd tell you that too."

This makes me think of the first time I came home with

my hair twisted in locks. The work had been done by my own hand, with no mirror and fingers caked with beeswax. The results were short, uneven, and pointing at the sky from my sloped scalp. It was far from the clean taper I'd worn for most of my eighteen years.

That had been the point, for me to do something different. I was a freshman in college, away from home and all of the thorned vines of the DC status quo. I was teaching myself patience by letting my hair undergo an initial metamorphosis into a new style. Everyone else got used to my locks and as they grew people even began to appreciate my new look. But not the Lone Ranger.

"I don't like them things you got in your hair," he had said to me. There was something in his tone that struck a chord inside me. I was my mother's child after all, so there was always the urge to seek approval. I always wanted to do the right thing for everyone, except for myself.

But I also knew that I was a man, and that a man has to stand his ground.

"I'm sorry you feel that way," I said to him. "But this is me."

He went quiet after that. I don't think he spoke to me for the rest of the visit. But it seemed like he got over it, until the next time he saw me, when we'd go through the exact same exchange. He even offered me several hundred dollars to cut them off one Fourth of July. But I still refused. It took almost seven years for him to figure out that my lengthening hair was there to stay. If that's what it was like for me, his "grandbaby," then I can only imagine what it must have been like to be one of his children, to be subject to that kind of scrutiny, that kind of stubbornness when it came to the more mundane things in day-to-day life: where you worked, who your friends were, or what time you came in at night. It was a house with laws not rules, laws that threatened severe punishments, both tangible and psychological, for those who disobeyed.

Yet Jesse Langley was not always the manipulator/ enforcer.

"I got to know him," Gary continues. "He liked life He liked living, even though his way of living wasn't about traveling or going places. He was happy just doing the things he liked to do. And he didn't like to do much. He was from the country. So all his life he worked. Then he'd have a little fun.

"He loved to take a drink, but he didn't drink all the time. He liked to sit around and watch the kids. He loved people. He was crazy about anybody. He didn't even have to know you to like having you around."

He liked having people around. Maybe that was why my mother's friends were always welcome, why so many kids from Trinidad showed up at the table for meals. Having lived with nothing but labor as a companion, he wanted to share his wealth with everyone he could. He wanted all to rejoice in the life he'd made for himself.

Gary was reared in the shadow of his father's protection and scrutiny. Following behind a scholar (Angela) and an athlete (Jesse, Jr.), it was hard for him to find his place within the filial hierarchy. But perhaps more important, it was hard for him to find his place in a neighborhood where no one seemed to be doing what they wanted, only what they had to.

Gary wanted to have fun. He wanted to be creative. He wanted every moment in his life to be his and only his. He wanted to make his own world in the very same way his father had made his own. And since his dad had provided so much without finishing school, there was no reason for Gary to continue. So he dropped out at sixteen and came of age in the drug-filled streets my parents somehow managed to avoid.

"I always wanted to play an instrument, but I never got a chance to do it. For some reason I could never get one to play. To this day I think that I should have been a musician. But I never got a chance to learn about music."

In his time there were no academic enrichment or free music programs in the summer, no college recruiters visiting his pre-dropout classrooms, not even older brothers and sisters cruising the block in Benzes and Beamers earned from jobs in the upper echelon of Black society. There was nothing to show him what his future could be.

Gary knew only what he saw: those men, like his father, who worked multiple jobs to keep all the bases covered, and the others who roamed the streets, making their living off of others.

"I was trying to find out what was going on. I wanted to know what was going on in the world, both worlds. So I got information from older cats. I was trying to figure out what I could do to not be in a bad way. I wanted to be able to weigh one thing versus another for myself."

It didn't take long for him to make a wrong turn on that expedition. Perhaps he poked his head between the wrong set of friends. Maybe some guy he looked up to told him that it was a cool thing to do. Take a pull on that joint. Pull those white lines toward your brain, or tap for a vein. However it came to be, that first surrender opened the floodgates for all that would follow. He grew into a young man trapped in a world viewed through lenses focused on nothing but his next fix.

He didn't start out palming the change from dressers and

open purses and "borrowing" the good silver. He didn't start out trying to sell the lawn mower my uncle Tony had under the rear porch for safekeeping. He would never have figured he'd be over fifty and still sleeping on a mattress in his parents' house, bound to his mother and the Lone Ranger, frozen in that adolescent funk of not knowing what to do in a world that only becomes ever more complicated.

"I don't know if it could have been avoided," he says about the drug problem that has never fully gone away. "It was what everybody was doing. We all tried it. I didn't know anybody who didn't in my peer group or the people who came before me."

Unlike many of his peers, at least he's still living. He didn't take his own life like his man Mike Reeves. I remember I was a little boy when Mike would visit the Langleys with his big Cazal frames and bushy beard. He once taught me never to lay a Bible on the floor because that was disrespectful. Angela still has a photo of him, Gary, and the Lone Ranger. Then some unnamed thing went down with Mike and a woman and he turned his own lights out.

Gary survived while all those faces went out of the shooting galleries in black bags, or remained among the living but with their brains fried forever. He's walked the old neighborhood blessed by the Creator himself. Never shot or stabbed. Never got too sick. Never took that jaw-breaking pipe to the face that my unnamed uncle earned for trying to hustle someone. Even when Gary did get busted for possession, the judge let him serve his time as a mentor in the prison's youth facility, where he bumped into my old boy Butchie Cunningham, who was still serving out his sentence for manslaughter.

In my view, the addict's story is always the same. It either keeps on going or it ends forever. There was the need for a few hundred for a detox that got spent before the program had begun. The nodding in the living room every other day of the week. The gradual decline of a once steadfast willingness to do what his mother and father asked him to. More than half a century and he's still scratching at slick walls, trying to climb up out of the abyss.

Thelma, his last girlfriend, told me that he'd shot up just before his father's funeral, that she opened the house's lone bathroom door and saw him there with the needle in his arm. But by then it wasn't that much of a surprise. By then I thought that he'd be the next to go, that his monkey would kill him before it would be pried free. It's good to see that I'm turning out to be wrong.

Jesse James Langley, Sr., believed in his favorite son longer than anyone else did. When the rest of us were suggesting that my grandparents put him out on his ass, he refused to uproot his own flesh and blood. He prayed and kept him housed and fed, despite the havoc wreaked on the quotient of valuables in the drawers and cabinets.

Once, up in his room, the Lone Ranger informed me that the Bible said a father should not abandon his child. And thus he was obligated to care for Gary as long as he had breath. Granddad made a similar statement when Tony moved to Atlanta with Jerome. In his mind grown men shouldn't live with other men, especially when neither seemed to spend much time with the opposite sex over the years. But still he let it be. Because that was what a father had to do, even if letting it be would do nothing in the end but reflect what he thought to be his own failures.

When it came to Gary, Jesse was always waiting on the manna from heaven, for his son to do a Lazarus and get his act together. After all, the father knew how to put down the bottle when he had to. And this was the son who was just like him, hardheaded but nobody's fool. He was certain that the boy would come around, and that the Lord would bless them both when he did. Too bad that gracious day never came, or at least not in the way the older man might have envisioned it.

"He left me with a lot of knowledge. When we talked we never talked no trash. We talked about these days, about what I should do when he died. He told me that day was coming. I used to hate to even talk about it, but he told me to accept it, that it was going to happen. 'I'ma have to leave you,' he'd say. 'I want you to know that.' He told me I was gonna be alright and I believed that. I'm gonna be alright."

Gary has a daughter he only learned about in recent years, Jeanette, a pretty girl who's a year older than me, with her father's face and complexion. Her mother, Caroline, kept his paternity a secret for more than twenty years. I walked into the house one Christmas and there she was at the dining room table, sitting there nervously, still uncertain as to whether or not she belonged.

"Jeanette got to know my father well, but she just came to see us late. I can't blame it on her. I blame it on her mother. Her mother had her thinking that somebody else was her father, that they were her family. And then she had to turn around in the middle of her life and find out who her real father was, who her real family was. She didn't know where that face in the mirror came from.

"I know that she wants to come around more than she does. But she's probably afraid. Because there's fear in the truth. The truth always scares people, whether it's good or bad."

Gary's life has improved considerably in the year or so

since that Fourth of July interview. Perhaps the Creator up above has finally answered our prayers for his deliverance. Perhaps he's begun to realize that there are more years behind him than there are ahead, that if he doesn't start living for anything other than a high, that there might be nothing left to signify that he was even here when he leaves.

He's more circumspect than his older brother and far less self-conscious than my mother. And he can still make us all laugh at a moment's notice. But that still doesn't change the horrors he's put us all through, most notably the stress that has often driven his mother to literal sickness. I love him as my mother's brother, yet, as with my uncle Mike before him, I'm not so sure I could ever trust him as a friend.

Gary now works for the DC Department of Sanitation and does his best to get his mother whatever she needs. He hit the Lotto and won five grand, much of which he gave to Jeanette to help her get a new home. He also led Sally Helen to her husband's grave on December 29, 2003, to commemorate the anniversary of his father's death.

I was there looking down at the brass plate bearing his name, fully aware of the irony that his spirit was looking down at it too from just above our heads. Sally Helen told him that she missed him, that we all missed him. My cousin Jay studied the four of our faces, unsure of how to react. My mother noticed a crack in the stone and let us all know that we'd stop by the management office to complain.

Gary just kept looking on without a word, his mind far away from any words we might have uttered. Perhaps his grief was deeper than all of ours combined. He'd lost his ace boon coon.

On the way out I watch what seemed like a hundred sparrows soaring wildly above the cluttered graves. Their mass morphed into more patterns than I could recognize. A spirit in the cemetery was restless. I only hoped it wasn't the one we'd come to see.

4

I am lying facedown in the rear of a black van. The seats have been removed for storage. The only window, heavily tinted, is high on the left wall. It is long after when I, barely six at the time, should be in bed.

I ride in relative quiet as the two brothers in front exchange words every few minutes, but mostly there's just the sound of the road beneath us, the gravel and asphalt that make the way from home to whichever "here" the driver has chosen. I am helpless. I am powerless. And I'm loving it.

Our destination finally arrives as the van slows to a stop. Not long after comes the reverberating thump of a bass line. Then come the drums, the bells, and finally a little guitar. The rear doors fly open and I'm nearly blinded by flashing lights in every color imaginable. I peer into the loading area and get a glimpse at the crowd. There are a million bodies moving, hands waving, voices clamoring, their combined energy bringing the fuse of my six-year-old senses to overload.

The younger brother assists the older in removing the red fur-covered turntables and speakers. They slide them onto wheeled skids to lighten the load and then push it all off into the madness. A moment later the door before me is shut tight and I fade into sleep, leaving my safety in the hands of the younger brother, Tony, as he backs us out of there. The older of the two, Jesse James Langley, Jr., aka "Junie," aka city-renowned

General Jay Jay on the ones and twos.

disco DJ General Jay Jay, is off to rock the designated crowd, not to be heard from again until the next time I happen to see him.

This is my first memory of my mother's oldest brother, the first time I can recall his taking me on any kind of journey. He's the Langley brother who's always been furthest from reach, the one who made his own rules while enforcing those of city and state, the one who in many ways escaped the Lone Ranger's grip by spinning and juking through every play.

Tall, slim, and as youthful as a man in his fifties can be, my eldest uncle is a master of image. His wavy hair is always freshly trimmed. His eyes and nose will always be just like his mother's. He changes cars every two years: the white on white in white Cadillac Seville, the '91 Corvette, the $90,000 convertible E-Class Mercedes. The leather pants and Italian kicks don't come cheap. Jesse, Jr., is always smooth, always ready to make his way to the center of a situation. Basically, he's everything his father was not. And that is probably the point.

In my years as nephew and grandchild, Junie's visits have always been the most brief. On Christmas he was always the last to arrive and the first to leave. He was the first to boast of my and his son's accomplishments, but the last to attend most of the events that made us who we are.

In the early years his yuletide gifts were almost exclusively new pairs of dress shoes, some in styles and shapes I often found myself too embarrassed to wear. The black Florsheims got worn for church every Sunday, but there was something about those brown snakeskin numbers I couldn't quite roll with. The same went for the brown rabbit coat he attempted to hand off to me after discovering it hidden deep within a closet somewhere in the Langley home.

Nevertheless I could never forget the actual journeys to Prince Georges Plaza shopping center to acquire those fabulous pairs of footwear. Every other counter girl knew him by name. And those who didn't wanted to. Ah, if only he'd been around more when I had that little virginity problem.

Yet my uncle Junie, before his recent marriage (and the other engagement that preceded it less than a year earlier), was not all ladies' man and scene stealer. His bravery and courage earned him a medal of honor in 1993, when he shot an escaping thief in the leg after a not-so-petty robbery. That's right. Junie was one of DC's finest.

"My favorite memory of Pops is the one I talk about all the time," he types on his end of our online chat connection. It was his idea for us to do the interview this way, so it'd be free. "It was him chasing those boys that stole milk from his truck."

Let me set the scene for you. A middle-aged Jesse parks his dairy truck across the street from his home and goes inside to eat the lunch his wife has graciously prepared. His seat in front of the small red-topped table facing the door gives him a perfect view of the milk-on-wheels he is charged with protecting.

It is summertime. All of his children are playing in the living room as he awaits Sally Helen's classic fried chicken, mashed potatoes, and whatever vegetable happened to be in season. But he's barely taken three bites when *they* walk into his field of vision.

Slang of the era, a "milk run" was defined as the act of finding an idling milk truck and jacking it for as much *leche* as one could carry without getting caught. For the kids it was a rite of passage. For the driver, depending on the severity of the hit, it could cost him his job.

Needless to say, "Big Jes" (as my mother called him) wasn't shaking those kind of dice. Picture the Lone Ranger in a white uniform with matching cap and apron. He jets out of his kitchen and through the front door so fast that the screen door nearly comes off its hinges. The perpetrators see him and do their Jesse Owens impression up past the rec center, toward the infamous Florence Hill, thinking that they will not be followed.

In your mind, maybe the old man catches one of them, probably the fat one or some fool trying to guzzle half the goods en route. But according to the accounts of three different Langleys, he got them all, plus every last carton back before they had ever been opened.

"Dad had jets. He was so fast!" Junie types, the excitement somehow radiating through the hum of my portable speakers.

I can only imagine what it was like to witness such a thing. Your father, the regular working guy, doing something so heroic, so extraordinary to a boy living in that boys' world of heroes and villains, cops and robbers. Your dad, the most nondescript man in the world, slides into a phone booth and emerges as just the opposite for all the neighborhood to see. Could this have been young Junie's inspiration for choosing to protect and serve?

"He used to love it when I told him that I wanted to 'be

like my daddy,' "Junie remembers. "Since I was the oldest boy
he expected so much out of me. He wanted for me to do a
lot of labor-type work, but I did more with my head than
anything else. I even wanted to go to college. But Dad was
unable to support Angela and me going to school at the same
time, so I went to the police force. I always wanted to help
people."

Junie was on the force for more than twenty years. In his
free time he worked closely with the DC Boys and Girls
Clubs and served as a track coach, helping to train high school
athletes in the sport in which he had always excelled. Even
now he rises before dawn to run and hit the weights, presses
and curls that produce more definition than my own body
will ever see.

His legs have taken him down many roads over the years.

A coat that only Junie could get away with.

Those paths have brought him through the Nation of Islam, the Prince Hall Masons, and the Republican Party. Though much of his history I've heard only from Sally Helen and my parents, there are photographs from his Masonic initiation, and I can remember that afternoon sometime in the mid-'80s when he strolled into the dining room and announced that he'd dumped the Democratic donkey for the regal Republican dumbo.

Junie has gone from cop to security guard to financier to part-time student, the title that makes him most proud.

"I'm finally in college," he says of the online associates degree program that first introduced him to cyberspace. "But this whole studying thing is hard," he admits. Currently living with Dottie, his wife of three years, in Lancaster, Pennsylvania, he's thinking of coming back home with his new degree, hoping to land a job with the Department of Defense or, if he's particularly crafty, the Department of Homeland Security. And if he's the Junie I know, he'll probably get a corner office his first week.

Yet this is all just the surface of the deceptively deep stream that is Jesse, Jr. From my vantage point his success, his demeanor, even the way he lives his life, are all part of his efforts to be autonomous, to remain free from the binds that snared the siblings that came before and after him.

"Junie has changed so much since we were little," Jackie declares. "He used to be a crybaby. Or at least he doesn't cry anymore the way he used to. He was the one the rest of us kids always got in fights with. He was the one who always showed up and upset everything."

Sally Helen will even tell you that he was the most temperamental of all the babies she bore. He was always crying, always angry. Growing up behind Daddy's little girl and before his father's favorite child, I imagine he was the one most starved for attention, the one most determined to turn heads out in the world, because they didn't turn at home. This, however, is far from saying that he did not have the deepest respect and love for the man after whom he was named.

"Dad was the greatest man of all time for a guy with a fifth-grade education," he marvels. "Everyone respected him in the hood because they knew how hard he worked. He saved all his checks from his job at the dairy and managed the family with the money he made from his second job as a cab driver.

"I remember he would always take me for rides in his car when he was going to Virginia and North Carolina. He always bought me a soda, and he always taught me that 'you can't have your cake and eat it too.' You have to work for what you get.

"The only thing that I wished my father had done that he didn't was to see me participate in sports. I think that's the reason I come down to see my son play so much."

Jesse's son is his spitting image. Tall and lanky, but with his mother's eyes, Jesse James Langley III was born on January 27, 1987. He was the first first cousin I knew, and the only one until Jeanette came into our lives. But in my eyes he's more like a little brother. Recently he informed me of his desire to attend my alma mater when he graduates from St. Alban's College High School in the summer of 2005.

"Lil' Jay," as we call him, plays whatever sport is in season. One of a handful of minorities at one of the city's most respected private schools, he's been struggling to fit in, to find his place in the world after a childhood full of movement.

Born of his father and Karen Faunteroy, a girlfriend from Junie's Boys Club days, Lil' Jay has spent most of his childhood

Lil' Jay at twelve, with his father.

being shuttled between his mother and paternal grandparents. As a matter of fact, his first years of school were at Ruth K. Webb Elementary, which his father and uncles attended long before him. He learned to ride his bike on the same blocks as Junie, Gary, and my father. But he'd also spend the weekends with his mother in Southeast and later P. G. County. But seeing his father beyond the fields and courts where he played was a rarity.

Junie would breeze through for dinner on Childress Street while Jay was still living with his grandparents. The two of them were more like distant cousins than father and son. Cordial greetings composed a conversation. There were few hugs. Maybe a handshake, maybe an "I love you." But they were not like my father and me, not best friends, not even major players in the stories of their lives. Junie dropped dollars, if anything at all, where guidance should have fallen. I can never forget the day that Jay turned to me after his father's departure. "Sometimes I hate him," he'd said. Jay was nine years old at the time.

I don't fully blame Junie. He was only emulating what he had seen. His father worked and came home. His money paid the bills. His words were law. His mother did as a wife should have and followed orders to a tee. This was life. This was what a man was to expect and what was expected of him.

"Dad got up in the morning fussing," Junie recalls. "When I was small I said to him, 'Daddy, why do you get mad every morning?' And he just laughed."

His parents were no Ozzie and Harriet. But as Junie grew it seemed as if the space between them widened whenever they sat on the couch together. The only time Junie saw them get close was when Sally Helen was handing his father dinner. How does that translate for a boy looking for someone to pattern himself after? How did that affect the way he dealt with the women who told him they loved him? Could it have had anything to do with the way he kept Karen at arm's length after their child was born? Might it be the reason that many of the beautiful sistas who could have been The One found themselves cast aside in the most passive-aggressive ways possible?

To me it seems as if my oldest uncle has been running one long race, one heat after the next in his flight from the person he didn't want to be. I think his infant cries were for an alternative to the life his father's footsteps might have dictated. So he donned a uniform marked with distinction and power. He spun disco hits that moved the masses from high above them, looking down on his musical constituents with regal glee. He drove fast cars fully loaded with the latest dime piece on the passenger side. He was determined to be everything the people in that house were not.

Yet as time burned by like the Old Man's squares, Junie remembered how he'd stood transfixed before that superhero chasing down the milk-stealing bad guys. He marveled at his old man's financial genius and the size of his treasure trove. He respected the Lone Ranger for always being there. Even during those long years of flight, I think he knew that he would eventually do the same.

"Dad had his faults," he says in his last line of our exchange in cyberspace. "But he was such a great man."

Something magical happened around the time Junie turned fifty. He jumped the broom at a Pennsylvania church to marry a woman he'd known since before Lil' Jay had come to be. He started going to church every Sunday and set his player card aflame. Lil' Jay goes up to visit, and Junie comes down for as many of his son's games as possible. He wants to give his son the support his own father was unable to give him, even if there have been more than a few potholes on the road to that dream. And my uncle still has that smile, that impervious grin that can con the toughest customer.

As I said before, I can't say that he and I have ever been close, though I remember his presence during moments that mattered. Being my Scorpio self, I'd always judged his motives and actions, always held him up to the level of conduct that I, even as a child, saw fit. I wanted him to be more like his father, even if I wasn't consciously aware of it.

I didn't figure it out until I looked at the scanty page that made up our interview. All my questions were answered in single sentences, with some subjects obviously avoided. There were things he would not say on the record, because I think he knows his father is still listening, still informing him of what he expects from the next realm. I have to respect that as his nephew, but for the writer trying to delve into the mysteries of the Lone Ranger, it provides only a thicker cloak of stealth.

In closing, I think of December 25, 2003, when Junie and I stood face-to-face in the dining room and actually conversed. It wasn't the usual light hug followed by quick exchanges, but a half hour of the pros and cons of online education, of the job markets here and up in the Keystone State, of the recommendation I will pen for his son no matter what college he applies to. We laughed and smiled and argued point for point, our mouths salivating from the scent of candied yams and Sally Helen's signature macaroni and cheese.

He is doing the best he can, and he knows that hasn't always been the case. But what's past truly is prologue. What is lost can only be remembered. Today is best seized before it burns to nothing, like a Lucky Strike in the fingers of a man he called "great," the first fellow he ever knew.

5

It's an unseasonably cold March day when I cross Sally Helen's threshold, wrapped in nothing but the used sport coat I've just snagged from the Salvation Army down the street. The beaming sun that morning had convinced me that warmth was on the way. I was clearly mistaken.

My grandmother wears a blue and white housedress, her silver hair perfectly combed and parted to the right. She's just finished cleaning the kitchen and is taking a break at the dining room table, the once crowded surface she now has all to herself.

"What did you say you needed again?" she asks me.

"Pictures," I tell her. "Old pictures of everybody."

The look on her face is one of confusion, as if to ask why I would need images of people I already know.

"It's for the book on Granddad," I say. Comprehension strikes like lightning.

"Oh, alright." She chuckles. "Go upstairs to the spare bedroom and look under the bed. There's a big plastic box. Bring it on down here."

Big is an insult to the size of the tub she speaks of. I need both arms to get it downstairs. Sally Helen looks on as I peel back the lid. The container is filled to the brim with nearly sixty years of snapshots.

I see my mother and father in matching corduroy coats on New Year's Eve, 1972. I see the beginnings of facial hair on Junie's face as he poses in a powder blue suit with a matching shirt and tie. There's the leather cap on Gary's teenaged head that reminds me of the ones some of my boys rocked back in grade school. A thirty-something Lone Ranger stands before a classic 1950s car on Florida Avenue, and a fortyish Sally Helen poses in a bathing suit and cap before a beachfront hotel in Nassau, Bahamas. I also happen to see a much younger version of myself decked out in a wide-collared shirt, brown vest, and pants, sitting between my Afro'd parents, back when we were one family instead of two.

But not one of those faces is most prominent in this mound of memories. Compared to a certain presence, all the other Langleys, Jaspers, Smiths, and Tysons are flashes in the pan. In the end, it's all about my uncle, baby boy Tony.

If Angela was the one who was always trying to do the

right thing, and Junie was the one doing his own thing, and Gary was the one unsure of which thing to do, then Tony was the one who did it all for his family. Sally Helen has proclaimed that he was the only child who didn't give her any pain.

Anthony Caesar Langley is undoubtedly his mother's favorite. Alternating between bouts of extreme quiet and a laugh so powerful that it can make a whole room double over, Tony

Uncle Tony as baby of the family.

is his mother's child in a family that mostly takes after Dad. This has made mother and baby son inseparable, a dynamic duo unlike any other in Trinidad.

"There was a big gap between Tony and the rest of the kids," Aunt Jackie says. "But Tony was Angela's shadow. He was our little brother and he went everywhere with us. It got so that we didn't even pay any attention to him. Sometimes he'd go back and tell Ms. Langley, and Angela would get in trouble."

He made his mark on the trails blazed by his older siblings, going wherever they would let him, playing their games and taking in all the words his head could hold. And then he went back home to report his findings to Sally Helen, the woman who still matters most in his life.

Like my father's brother Mike, Tony came of age in Trinidad just as its blocks began to dim. But Tony's tale is without divorce, addiction, or baby-mama drama. Tony has made a wonderful life for himself, even if it isn't necessarily the one he dreamed of.

"I wanted to grow up and become a doctor," he begins as we're driving toward his new home in Henrico County, Virginia, with his friend Jerome. The condo is less than an hour from Powhatan and ninety minutes from the streets of the boyhood he left behind.

"But I didn't do it because I didn't finish college like I should have. If I had to do it all over again I might not have become a doctor, but I would've gone on to finish college, maybe to have become a teacher."

Tony did graduate from Spingarn High School. It is his picture that I remember most vividly in the Langley dining room, hanging on one side of the archway leading to the family room. There he is, smirking proudly with a trimmed 'fro and mutton chops, the very image of innocent youth. Now, some thirty years later (and probably as many pounds heavier), he hasn't changed much: he is five nine; has his mother's complexion, big brown eyes, and lips that purse just so.

Of all my uncles, Tony is without a doubt my favorite as well because he has always been there. I can never forget the blinding beam from his Super 8 camera at nearly every birthday I had from one to thirteen. His gifts were the largest and most elaborate at Christmas, though in typical grown-up fashion I can't remember exactly what he gave me until after I became a man, and then it was all sweaters and shirts. But I do know that it was he who drove to my parents' home on Christmas Eve to deliver my gifts just after I'd fallen asleep, trying to wait out Santa out on the living room sofa. It was he who drove Mom, Grandma Sally, and me when we went to a mall. It was he who was always there for dinner during my visits to Sally Helen and Jesse's on those Sundays long ago.

From his late teens on into his thirties, Tony was a faithful employee of C&P, Central and Pacific Bell, the local telephone company. When it split with AT&T he went over to the long-distance end of things, answering calls and fielding reports until he moved up the management ladder. Then, circa 1994, he hit the glass ceiling in his local office. With no college degree but carrying plenty of praise for

Tony wearing his classic grin in Sally Helen's kitchen.

his work, he was given a choice when his office got downsized: He could take the severance package like everyone else, or he could take a new position in Atlanta. He packed his bags.

Tony pulled into Hotlanta halfway through my freshman year of college. His apartment was almost an hour away from Morehouse's campus. Yet I saw him whenever I needed him. He fronted me money when the writing gigs I lived on ran thin. He drove me out to the suburbs of Stone Mountain to shop, where grocery prices were cheaper. After I got my own car, he offered me a meal and his washer and dryer on those Sundays when drawers and socks were in short supply. He exploded into tears on the eve of my college graduation, as the entire family (sans Gary and the Lone Ranger) raised glasses of sparkling cider in celebration.

During those years Tony and Jerome were my family away from the family. Even later, when I returned to the ATL for two book tours, Tony was there in the first row, sitting ahead of the only other two people present. Now he's living in Richmond, because of another promotion, and the need to be closer to his mother, particularly after his father's death.

I could sense the trepidation in his voice the first time I mentioned my wish to interview him for my book project. Though he can be quiet, his role as his mother's protector is as conspicuous as the tuft of wavy hair he combs backward to cover his slowly expanding bald spot. Airing dirty laundry isn't his style. So I know that the answers he gives will be careful, perhaps too careful.

"He was a very good father to me," he declared. "He always gave me what I wanted, and whenever I needed something he was there for me. He didn't really have any failures.

"He was a fun-loving party-type man who loved to have fun. He loved music and to dance. On Sundays he would always take us for rides to Baltimore, and in the summers we'd go to Carl's Beach, which was the Black beach. He would go and listen to the music and I would get in the water. I remember we even went fishing for herring once. He made the nets for us to catch the fish, and we had a lot of fun, even though we didn't catch anything."

It's hard for me to picture little Tony and the Lone Ranger rod-and-reeling it like in the opening of *The Andy Griffith Show*. It's even tougher to picture the old man cutting a rug to music down by the shore with cute little Tony doing the dog paddle off in the distance.

My reflections on father and youngest son are of Tony taking one arm, Junie the other, as they led a drunken Jesse, Sr., in nothing but his drawers, back up to his room during the opening of Christmas presents. I remember that Thanksgiving dinner when baby son demanded silence from his daddy dearest. But most of all I remember the two of them barely being on the same plane, ships always passing each other in an ocean the size of a three-bedroom townhouse. Tony can't be telling me the whole truth. He just can't be.

"He was a man of few words," Tony goes on. "And the only time you could really sit down and talk with him was when he came home from work. Because after he came home and ate he went right to sleep."

I ask my favorite uncle what he thought of his parents' marriage and he dodges the question completely.

"He taught me to work for what I want," he says, "and he was a father who was home when many of the others in the neighborhood weren't. They had left their wives and all of that. He was the way he was because he came from the old school where the man was supposed to do everything and make all the decisions. Ma was the one who was always home with us while he was out working. But we were a closer-knit family than any of the other ones I knew. We ate dinner together every night at the same table. That's the one thing we've always done as a family."

Tony and my mother are the ones who work the hardest to keep Langley tradition alive. He drives from Richmond to DC practically every weekend to look in on his mother, and does a large amount of the cooking since Sally Helen can't get around the way she used to. He's also at work on building a home for his mother on the land she owns in Powhatan, the stretch of property that once held the glorious Smith residence before it burned to the ground.

He does all this in the humblest manner, reserving words for only when they're needed, or when he can make us all laugh. As a boy I often dreamed that Tony would one day get married and give me the coolest little cousins to play with. He would be the best father a child could have. But thus far it doesn't seem to be in the cards.

"There it is, Daddy," he'd said in the back of the limousine as we drove from the wake to the funeral. The car slowed before 1341 Childress for the departed to give the home he'd inhabited one last good-bye. It was the only time I'd ever heard Tony call the Lone Ranger "Daddy."

The man's passing had given his youngest son the freedom to finally call him what he was, as if the two of them were making peace after a long silent war. Just then I wanted to put a hand on Tony's shoulder, to tell him that it was going to be all right as he cried on the inside, but I also knew it was best to leave him be.

6

"The one thing you have to understand is that he didn't have much of a childhood," my mother says somewhat solemnly, her eyes cutting toward something beyond the lime green wall where I'm seated.

Rain patters against the high window to her left on the Saturday after her fifty-fourth birthday. This is the second time I've put a mic before her on the same subject, but it doesn't bother her in the least. She's always happy to share with her only son.

"He was nine or ten when he had to get out in the fields and work for his grandparents. So he never really learned things like sports. So he was very traditional. We all sat and ate together and went to bed at the same time. That meant it was a really big thing when we got a TV. As a matter of fact I think he thought the TV took a lot of attention away from him, even though he loved *Bonanza*. And he was the kind of person who needed attention because he'd spent most of his younger years not getting it."

I can imagine how it went back then, him crossing that threshold in the gray uniform with the white apron across his waist, that outfit that Sally Helen has washed and pressed as if her life depended on it. Dinner is waiting, as are the children, for the king of the castle to sit down for the family meal. The Lone Ranger believed in the America of old, in that concept of family made visual by Norman Rockwell. Work hard and come home to a good meal, before you lie down and get up to do it all over again. The '60s chipped away at our so-called great nation's faith in that ideal. By the '80s, it'd been completely overturned.

Knowing those things, it's not hard to understand why the Lone Ranger would be enamored with the story of a man and his sons working hard to turn a buck in the Old West. Minus my mother, the paradigm fits pretty perfectly. The Lone Ranger is Ben Cartwright. Junie is Adam. Gary is Hoss, and Tony, of course, is Little Joe, with Sally Helen playing Hop Sing, the cook. I can see him sitting there on that green velour couch, giving in to the idiot box for the given hour before bed. The next morning he would continue his less glamorized version of the working life behind the wheel of a milk truck. Because like Ben Cartwright, he would always be a provider.

"He was always working," Angela continues, "so he didn't really go to a lot of PTA meetings and things like that." But that didn't mean he didn't do his best to help his children with their studies. "There's this book his grandfather gave him, that I still have," she continues, "and when I was really young he taught me this poem that's in there." She recites it as if she were seven all over again. Same smile, same gleam on that broad Langley forehead:

Friends with joy
We welcome you.
We greet you one and all.
We thank you for your presence here
Both great and small.
We know you've come to hear us speak
And see us act our parts.
We'll try to do our very best
With glad and loving heart.
We hope you will be entertained.
We'll strive to please each one.
And when the evening's over I trust you'll say well
     done.

"He would sit there every time I had to learn something for school and have me say that poem first. I've actually taught it to some of my kids at school over the years. Because I knew that he took pride in that poem. He didn't graduate from high school but I always felt he was wise. He was good with figures too. So when I was in high school and they'd started teaching the modern math, he would try his best to help me."

The snow in those winters seemed whiter, less contaminated by the pollution that now poisons everything in our techno-freak world. While little Melvin and his crew were out on that big hill sledding, the Lone Ranger was making his kids vanilla snow cones with the powder from his very own yard. He played checkers with all four kids, giving them all shots at the title until they got tired of losing. He went fishing with his friends and brought home the spoils, though Junie would always find an excuse not to eat the catch of the day.

He took the family for those famous rides on Sundays and down to the motorcycle racetrack in southern Maryland where, for a dime each, he paid for all four kids to zoom the concourse as they held on tight to the designated drivers. And there were the summertime sojourns to Cars and Sparrows beaches, where Black boys and girls could have the time of their lives, even if half of the rides made Junie sick. Like Tony said, his dad liked to have fun.

Still, fun in the Lone Ranger's house was overshadowed by rules. And those rules were many. Not only did you have to be in the house at a certain time and go to church every Sunday, but there were other, more important things that you had to understand.

"He had a lot of what some would consider old values about how things had to be done," she recalls. "I remember my great-grandmother William-Anne Langley used to say that a child should never look an older person in the face, that you weren't supposed to make eye contact. So I was afraid to look at her.

"So a lot of how he behaved had to do with his understanding of the level of respect for elders that has always been prevalent in the Black community. That you just don't come into a house without saying hello and being welcomed by the eldest person in the home."

So my mother's sending me up to see him was part of my training. She wanted me to understand that age translated into power. At almost eighty-four he'd lived far beyond almost everyone he'd ever known, and he didn't mind reaping the benefits.

"Even though he was quiet, he really was a people person. He liked for the whole family to be there. He tried to act like it was no big deal, but he loved the Fourth of July and Labor Day and everybody coming together to eat. He really loved his family."

There was a time, presumably in the mid- to late '50s, when both of my grandfather's older brothers, Willie and Frank, came to live in the Langley compound. Eight people were packed into a three-bedroom home without anyone feeling uncomfortable. Willie made it his job to keep the grown-ups laughing while Frank used his comic skills to keep the kids giggling. Here was little brother Jesse, a father and homeowner who could provide not only for his family, but for the brothers he'd left behind in Greenville when he came to DC to seek his fortune. It made him proud, even if his brother Frank, whom he visited every Sunday until his death in 1999, wasn't living the life he would have chosen for him.

"They would go back and forth about the fact that Frank used to drink a lot and that sometimes Dad wasn't pleased with some of the women he would see Frank with." They tended to be loud, or drunk, unladylike, or a combination of the three.

Those who say that hypocrisy is the greatest sin might have burned Jesse Langley, Sr., at the stake. As Mom's words register, I see those drums of rum and gin on the floor by his mattress. I can smell the liquor on his breath as I kiss him on the cheek. From where I stand, outside of their time, the older brother was just as bad as the younger. Then again, the Lone Ranger kept his habit in check, whereas Frank, as the man getting it together under Little Brother's roof, did not. Frank eventually left his brother's home and ventured back out into the world's wilderness, where he was overcome by a stroke and left just a tad shy of being a vegetable until his death, at eighty, in 1999.

There's a framed photo in my bedroom of the two of them, taken less than a year before Frank's passing. Jesse is cutting his big brother's hair as Frank sits slumped over, a little brother taking care of the one who came before him. For a moment, I think about myself, about all the things that can filter through a bloodline: genetic tendencies and character traits, addictions, projections, and displacements. I think of the times I watched my mother say one thing and do another, of the way she chastised me for what I was too young to see as her own failures.

Then I think of my short life, of the friends and lovers I have openly judged despite my own outlined flaws. Maybe it came from him, just like the narrow size-twelve's that are a pain to find shoes for. Maybe he and I are more alike than I ever would have thought. After all, he and Mom are far more similar than she would ever want to admit.

"I have to readily admit that he spoiled me," she laughs, exploring the departed in her mind from where we sit. "I was the only girl and the oldest, and I had had an older brother before me who died. So I think I was really special to him. There was this story he used to tell me about when I was a baby and he was taking me out for a walk. Then out of nowhere this thunderstorm came and he pushed me into the closest building, which was the Sears and Roebuck that used to be on Bladensburg Road, so I wouldn't get caught in the storm, so that nothing would happen to me.

"But I would always say that I was nothing like him when I was teenager and I had started dating. Because back then I was scared of him. There would be times when I'd want to go downtown on a Saturday with my friends, but I'd be afraid to ask. So I'd end up doing things like leaving a note on his dresser and hoping that that would be okay. When we went to the dances they would have in the rented-out hotel room downtown he'd always end up dropping us off or picking us up so he'd know that we were where we were supposed to be. I guess he just didn't want me to grow up too fast."

Angela Marilyn Langley Jasper still believes in so much of what her father instilled in her. She still carries the name Jasper. She believes that what's right is right and that you shouldn't half-step anything. She believes in paying the bills and saving money, though she's had some trouble here and there. And like him, she didn't believe in divorce. Married people were supposed to stay together.

Her father never talked to her about the kind of man she should look for. Their conversations never even hinted at his view of a woman's role in a household. It's even my mother's hypothesis that her father's departure from Sally Helen's bed was due to the fact that she had started working again after the better part of twenty years as a homemaker.

Much like him, my mother didn't do a lot of dating before she married. Much like him, she was always with one person. The more I look at her, the more I see his features. Now she's the one coming to Childress to check on things. She's the one who signs the checks. She's become the person her mother depends on most. She's somehow filled so much of the void her father left behind.

There's no rhyme or reason to being a provider. All you know is that nothing's for free. Dinner ain't so delicious when the fridge is empty, and the kids don't study as well when they've got holes in their shoes. What you want goes on the fire to keep the family warm. Maybe that's why he found pleasure in little things: a smoke and a drink, a change into comfortable clothes to catch a breeze out on the porch. What I saw as an angry hermit's life was merely the ending of a long life of work, one with little time to sit and enjoy the breeze, and no room to sit in a chair at the front of the house and think to himself. Life had slowed down for a man who'd never known slow, and after what seemed like a long fight, he finally chose to sit back and be an old man.

"He told me a lot of things that I didn't understand as a young child," she says. "But I understood them as I grew older. If I was having trouble with something, he would say, 'Rome wasn't built in a day.' No elaboration, no explanation, as if the phrase could speak the same volumes to the child as it did to the adult."

"Marriage ain't a bed of roses," he'd once remarked. There's no way he could've known just how poignant those words would be for his firstborn.

"He took heed to good advice and learned a lot as a result of the conversations he had with people in his cab," my mother pointed out. "And he always stayed close to politics. He read everything there was when Martin Luther King died and anything that had to do with Lyndon Johnson. But the thing that really sticks out in my mind about him is that he always wanted us to get the best and to do the best. If you're gonna get a pair of shoes, get a good pair, even if that's the only pair you're gonna have. And he always wanted us to watch the company we kept. He wanted us to 'be with somebody that really wants to be somebody.' "

It is in this moment that I know how hard it is for her without the man up in the back room. I can feel that, as one of the few left to care for the Lone Ranger's widow, she often is lost. I understand that her visits to him were trips to an older version of herself seeking advice and absolution from the one who paved the way for all that she achieved: two degrees, a little boy, and the knowledge that she will not be forgotten by those she educated.

"He was always there for me," she says, on the verge of a sob. "I never remember being cold or without food. He was a good provider."

7

No one will talk about the downside of Jesse Langley, Sr. Tony went as far as to say there wasn't one. Junie has ignored the question. Gary knows the dark side of which I speak but will not elaborate, and my mother speaks in cryptic phrases. She will imply, but not specify. I have to find answers. I have to speak to someone who knew him before Childress Street and before the Pentagon, someone who knew that young boy back in Greenville, North Carolina, who lost his folks. Someone who knew him when the fields served as the border for all that he understood. I'm sure there were many such *someones* once. But the question now is who's still living. I'll need to look, but first I have to deal with the situation at hand.

No one in their right mind should show *ER* in an actual emergency room. But there it is, blaring from the four screens pointed in each direction. I've been here for five hours, standing, sitting, and pacing in a structure that seems light-years away from the New York I know. A man twice my size has pulled himself into the fetal position to accommodate the lack of space on the couch he's lying on. The woman at the front desk munches on a box of KFC honey-barbecue wings. And

I, having returned from my trip with Dad through the old neighborhood barely two days ago, am slumped over in my pleather seat, waiting to hear something.

My stomach's filled with nothing but Starbursts and Reese's cups and I haven't been sleeping well. I am waiting for the verdict. A vivid imagination produces some doctor announcing cancer, AIDS, Ebola, or other worst-case scenarios. Five hours is too much time to be left waiting. It gives my imagination twenty acres' worth of prognostications.

Then a phone line comes alive at the front desk. A moment later I am being escorted beyond the NO ADMITTANCE doors to where she's being kept. My woman is sandwiched between two people in far worse shape. One, an overweight white man, wears a bandage across his abdomen. The other, an elderly Black woman, moans in pain. She's just sitting there reading one of those mass market fantasy novels she can't get enough of, her glasses perched on the edge of her nose, as if the cramps haven't been killing her for the last four days.

Her period hadn't come, and she had no medical insurance. I got the phone call and was begged to travel from Brooklyn to Long Island because she didn't want to go to the hospital alone. We'd been fighting and I was tired of the same shit every other day. I had been looking for a way out.

She smiles a perfect smile the minute she sees me. She's been alone through all the questions and blood work, and all the waiting. Now I'm here and things are looking better.

"So what's the deal?" I ask, pretending to be calm, playing the role of the one who has to keep the both of us from losing it as she stands to her feet, wanting to make sure that I hear her perfectly.

"I'm pregnant," she says. My mind immediately scrolls through every interlude of the past few weeks.

I'm confused. There were no breaks, no spills, no slipping it in for a sec and pulling out just in time. My dad had me rolling rubbers on bananas before I even knew what a vagina looked like. So I don't get it. I can't speak, so I pull her to me, bringing her heart to my own. Somewhere within the grid-lock of panic, I begin to feel, of all things, joy.

I told myself that, last time, with that last woman, that I'd run out of excuses, that if one of my little sperm made an egg connection there would be no questions, no discussions, no weaseling out of what my father describes as the greatest job he's ever held (and the one he's best at). Now the event has arrived. Now we have to deal with it.

I immediately give this new thing within her all the prop-erties of myself. I see it toddling up the hallway for a plate of Mom's pancakes while Dad sprays Pledge on the woodwork with John Coltrane playing in the background. I watch it sail down W Street during its maiden voyage on a two-wheeler without training wheels. I try to imagine which art it will in-herit from one or both of us, the color of its eyes, the size of its skull. I am presenting it freshly born to spanking-new grandparents who never thought such a thing would happen so soon. Truth be told, this is what I've been waiting for. This is my silent prayer finally made real.

Then I remember my bank balance, followed by the re-minder that she's in her first year of law school, followed by the realization that things have been far from kosher as of late. I think of a man I once called a friend and the gray area he continues to inhabit as a "baby-daddy," only able to see his lit-tle girl when Mom says so. This is not the best of times. But the clock keeps on ticking.

I can't picture what an abortion was in Sally Helen's time. Maybe taking a fall off a horse or begging your man to give you a swift kick to the gut. In reality those things would've been pleasant in comparison to the available medical versions of the procedure. More than likely it wasn't much of a thought at all, not for a farming family, who could always use more hands in the fields, even if it meant another plate to fill at the table 365 days a year.

For a woman in Sally Helen's day, not having a child was like not learning how to walk. I imagine that as being even more of a certainty for young Jesse James Langley, a boy who jumped to man before he could spell either word. He and his brothers had given up their childhoods for the sake of providing for the family. My grandfather would have wanted to play a part in giving a newborn what he never got to have.

And he'd want to do it over and over again in hopes of living vicariously through his piece of the future. Family was a guarantee unless you'd been cursed by the Lord Almighty. Sure, there were a good number of cursed ones, but you didn't chat about it in mixed company. I can't imagine the pain of multiple miscarriages, of knowing that two bodies could fail at their most important task time and time again. I know that it happened to my grandparents, yet they eventually prevailed.

My mother and her brothers were a blessing to two kids who thought that they might be cursed, that they could be real-life evidence that the story of Job could be true. They were a man and woman on the edge of their twenties when my mother came into the world. Everything in the nigger-hating world they knew said that a good job and a house they owned were as good as it got, a perfect roll of the dice with an endless number of sides. They were the lucky ones.

Yet two generations later, I, the fruit borne of their efforts, don't feel so lucky as I embrace the gift that they for many years thought might elude them. I see a Draconian health-care system and splitting my checks for one three ways. I see cramped living spaces at ballooning prices. I see an unreliable girl who burns through dough like kindling. I'm more afraid than I was when a certain young man put a gun to my head at seventeen just to see how tough I was. But I have to get through it.

I multiply this feeling times five and I see why the Lone Ranger never stopped working, never stopped saving, never stopped looking as far down the road as his chocolate eyes could stretch. And I can see why there was such a downside when his armor wore thin.

I've got a kid on the way, which means I could potentially nose-dive into that pit of mediocre family relations that so many of my peers cavort in like pigs in slop. And that once again brings back my father's words. My generation has even more choices than his did; some of these choices are killing our community each and every day. And no, I'm not digress-ing. Let me backtrack.

Let's take it back to slavery for a moment, back to the four hundred years of oppression every clichéd angry Black man drops in the latest buddy movies at the local cineplex. Let's take it back to the four centuries during which our lives were not our own, when millions met their end in the jaws of sharks, or at the bottom of the Atlantic Ocean. Let's revisit fa-thers separated from children and the women they made them with.

The disobedient were whipped to the bone, tortured,

maimed, and humiliated in front of the little scraps of community they had managed to retain. Riots were ratted out by brainwashed sycophants hoping for a little more gravy to go with their leftover biscuits. There would be no more of our native religion. Familial histories were destroyed. Life meant working for someone else without pay, and working without pay for a pink-skinned owner was the very definition of Black life.

When a child was born there was still celebration. The community saw the need for that little being to be shown the way. Jesse's grandparents, Drew and William-Anne Langley, were two of those children, and they raised the Lone Ranger in that tradition. The same went for Lucy and Robert Smith, Sally Helen's folks. From their learning, a parent's role was to do whatever it took to keep things going, to do whatever was needed to ensure that there was a tomorrow not only for the family, but for the community as well.

Of course this wasn't always the case. Selfishness and envy are as old as the world. Confusion and ignorance are the most effective tools of the darker forces. The Great Migration was the first chink in the armor. Unemployed men with ever-growing families headed north to find work in factories or west toward the shipyards and aircraft companies in California. They ventured forth, planning to send money home for their people, and eventually to send for the people themselves. But that did not always happen.

Some of those men started new families. That girl at the after-work dance hall with all that junk in the trunk became a better prospect for wifey than the old ball and chain back at the crib. New money brought new material things to aspire toward, things that the new women swooned over and desperate men killed for. Those who crapped out in the job lines

started working angles in the streets, angles that eventually became rackets, and rackets that ultimately grew into our own
little underworld.

This is not to say that there weren't tens of thousands of
families reunited above the Mason-Dixon Line. It only con-
firms the beginnings of fissures in our community that would
burst apart in generations to come. By the '50s and '60s, as
Tony observed, single-parent homes weren't hard to come by,
and Black folks all over found themselves free men and
women still at the very bottom of the totem pole. The ghetto,
as we came to know it, was born.

By the '70s, the Black Power and the women's movements
had a head-on collision. Heroin flooded the streets. Malcolm
and Martin were silenced. Basically all hell broke loose. And
instead of channeling all our power toward those pulling the
strings that controlled our oppression, we pointed our
weapons at each other, at our own men and women, at our
brothers and neighbors. And it was the children, my generation, who took it all in.

What we grew up witnessing was a world where everybody did what they wanted and complained about it later. We
saw those who went home drunk from the club "Amen"
themselves to death in the front pew a few hours later. A lot
of us saw our father blow through the family house a few
times a month, whenever he wasn't tied up with the woman
he was with or out in the streets living it up like we didn't
need him. And we saw our mother tell lies about how we
came to be, about why the man who had helped make us had
become a complete stranger.

Our heroes became anyone who had dough, no matter

how he got it. And our only salvations were government checks and Powerball when the jackpot got real big. No one told us about our past, not even about those who had come a generation or two before us. We came into a Reaganized world unarmed and unprepared for the forces arrayed against us.

So now fatherhood has become dropping off that check whenever we have it while casually mentioning to whichever woman we meet at the bar that we have a son or a daughter. The picture in the wallet is often old and dated. And that kid learns the word *daddy* only after he's started to speak in full sentences. Among women the move is to find the dude with the most to offer, the freshest car and clothes, and see what they can get from him, hoping that what he has to offer will be enough.

This is not a rant, but a list of the realities that have passed before my eyes for as long as I can remember. Yet I refuse to make these things part of the future for that little life growing inside of my lady. I will work like the Lone Ranger before me to build a fortress to protect that child's potential. I will find a way to shell out the five figures a year necessary to make sure every cell of his or her intelligence is harvested properly. I will provide until the heart in my chest throws in the towel, because that is what a father does, and now a father is what I am.

My life is no longer about me and my sexual needs, nor does it concern my desire to feel free and handle my business without some woman stressing me. I know I have my faults: a short temper, biting wit, and the patience of a speed freak when it comes to foolishness. I am slow to forgive and quick to judge and I don't like to dress up to do my job.

But none of these things will stop me from fulfilling my role as half of this child's source of protection and support. None of this will hold me back from doing what my great-

great-granddad might have done for a child he never saw again.

My woman and I hold hands as a taxi drives us off into the Long Island night. It is hard to breathe knowing that I have so much to live up to, so much to come to understand in nine months' time. If I'm to follow in the steps of the Lone Ranger, while also trying to build a better family for myself, then I need to know all I can about those who taught him, about the place that made him what he was.

My woman tells me she loves me. I pull her to me, fatigue pushing my eyes into slits. There's a long hard road ahead but I will make it. We will make it.

country boy

1

The Rotten Apple tries its best to keep you from leaving. Thus, getting out is more of an escape than a departure. I'm in my '88 CRX with a slow leak in the rear left tire, on the way to discover a piece of the Lone Ranger's past.

Exact directions are scribbled on a crumpled piece of notepad. But I just *have* to follow them in my own arrogant way, ignoring my cousin's advice and taking another route altogether. Thus I end up creeping along the FDR, a slave to both rubbernecking and the geriatric woman going twenty-five mph in the passing lane. When I finally do get to the GW Bridge, the only exit for Interstate 95 is leading in the opposite direction. So I have to hop off in the Bronx, make a fistful of unexpected turns, and switch to the scenic Henry Hudson Parkway with only ninety minutes (based on my projected arrival time of 3 p.m.)

to make it to a town with a name I can't remember in another state, following directions designed for use via another thoroughfare entirely. Needless to say I get lost.

An hour later I've consulted an old map in the glove box and know exactly which way to go. But the Richter scale in my stomach reads about a 6.5, which means it's time for a food run.

I'm the only speck of color inside the food complex. Super-suburban eyes scan me from all around, particularly the red-haired clerk at the meat counter, who seems reluctant to give me the two pieces of heat-lamped fried chicken I need to gorge my hunger. An hour ago I was driving past corner-side checker games and bulletproof-glassed carryouts. Now I'm in *their* America, the one the Lone Ranger knew far better than I, the one that he knew from birth would always be his enemy.

A beat later I am back on the road to Oz, thinking of how different my experience is from most. For me, a child of Chocolate City, it was always the white folks who were the minority. It was they who came to our malls and movie theaters, knowing that they'd always be outnumbered on our side of town. As a little boy I never thought of them as some imperial threat, as descendants of the people who had committed unspeakable atrocities against us. To me, back then, they just needed a suntan, and maybe a little more seasoning in their staple dishes.

Now, driving through this great wide open called Westchester, I cringe to think of what my life would've been like had my mother delivered me in this kind of somewhere else, this seemingly endless expanse of estates and country clubs that only a few of us ever gain access to. My skin crawls at the thought of living in a place where I'd have to pander to a community that feels entitled to having the world as their oyster because their ancestors planted a flag on someone else's soil. At least I came into a world where my parents could legally choose to rear me wherever they liked. For my grand-father there was only where he was and the short list of other towns, cities, and states where colored people could go.

My cousin Willie "Bruh" Langley, Jr., is the oldest of the five brothers who moved to Norwalk, Connecticut, from their home in Greenville, North Carolina. They are the Lone Ranger's nephews, the offspring of his half-brother Willie, Sr. My father endearingly refers to Bruh and Co. as "The Gyp-sies" because of their notorious habit of blowing by 1341 Childress with less than a day's advance notice.

I've met the Norwalk brothers three times before this visit, once a few months earlier on an Easter Sunday at my grand-mother's, and another time years before, at our first "family re-union," which took place in the parking lot of some less than plush motel near Greenville. The refreshments that day con-sisted of buckets of chicken and chitlins. The entertainment came from my then six-year-old cousin Jay running around the parking lot as if he were being chased by unseen enemies. My last meeting with the brothers was at the Lone Ranger's funeral.

Earth, Wind and Fire's "Reasons" plays on my stereo as I cross the Connecticut border forty minutes behind schedule. I always remind myself that the song is not the lofty love bal-lad many assume it is, but a relatively shallow confession about a one-night stand and the emptiness that follows. The lyrics dictate the story very succinctly.

He looks at *her* in a sultry club. Her body is just right. Her lips curl into the most inviting smile, one he wants to own, for the night. But in the morning, when the afterglow has long faded and there's nothing to consider but the day ahead, there is nothing left but vague memories, no feeling to complicate the life of a soul brother smack in the middle of the '70s.

The interlude, in the end, was just something to do after the disco. Rather shallow for classic soul, but very reflective of the times. I'm kind of ashamed I was in my mama's belly at the time she and my father attended the concert where the live version of the single was recorded.

I follow the directions to a red two-story with a sloped driveway. A gleaming white Ford pickup sits in front, its silver rims sparkling as if they're fresh out of a hip-hop clip.

Bruh is standing in the doorway before I reach it. He is still wearing his black slacks and white shirt from church, and his balding head almost reaches the top of the doorframe. Just then he seems like the biggest member of my family, with a paunch concealing the shiny buckle on his belt.

"So I see you finally made it," he says. I laugh in embarrassment and we hug before going into the house.

His home is everything I would expect of a father and grandfather. A framed copy of the commencement bulletin from his daughter Renee's law school graduation hangs in one corner, as do a series of artificial flower bouquets attached to a mirrored background. Renee now lives in Atlanta and has two kids of her own. She always comes to see me on my book tours.

On the table is a stack of photo albums, which Bruh begins to show me one at a time. Many of the images feature him with the many cars he's owned over the years. (At present there's the pickup and a '98 Lexus LS400.) There is also a shot of Junie taken back when he was General Jay Jay, complete with his signature turntables covered in red fur. The pic-

ture slightly resembles the one above it, of a young Bruh doing the twist at a party.

Bruh's second wife, Tina, is out of town and his eldest son,
Rodney, has borrowed the Lexus for a friend's wedding. Paranoid after my less than smooth journey, I quickly assume there
is no one else around, that despite his promises in the course
of our previous conversations, he will be the only one I have
to interview. He bursts my foolish bubble a moment later
when he tells me not to start anything yet, because we're
about to take a ride.

It's a five-minute cruise to his younger brother James Marvin's abode, a colonial with a two-car garage and multiple automobiles in the back. In his driveway are a '99 Honda Civic,
a truck, a '98 Lexus GS300, and a motorcycle. We park and
walk around to the rear of the house, where they're all waiting for us.

Hugs and hands are exchanged freely, even before Bruh
introduces me to the trio of men sitting in lawn chairs surrounding a white plastic table. Ashley, James Marvin, and
Donnie are three of Bruh's five living brothers. Donnie, their
nephew, is also there. The next-door neighbors—a daughter
adding extensions to her elderly mother's mane—say hello
and wave to me, the obvious visitor, from across the driveway.
I wave back. It's a lovely summer afternoon, even if the skies
are white, indicating that rain could be a-coming.

The only parties missing from among the original Langley brothers are Curtis and their other brother, Doug, who
passed away in 2003 due to complications from diabetes.

"Curtis is probably off somewhere saving the world," Bruh
jokes about the man who never stops talking. I learned this on
the night before the funeral, when the spectacled peanut-

colored man went on for close to an hour about his daughter Latanya, an attorney, and all the things she's contributed to the world in her twenty-eight years. She and I are the same age, yet we've never met.

Ashley nearly hits the floor when he realizes who I am— Angela's son and Sally Helen's grandson! The Langley brothers hold both mother and daughter in the highest regard. "You're Angela's son?" he asks in his refined and almost scholarly voice. "How old are you?"

"Twenty-eight," I say. He seems awed.

They all look at me with a kind of endearment I don't understand. Sure we're related, but I didn't see these faces at my junior-high graduation or my first poetry reading. They weren't there for the barbecues and birthday parties, and they don't appear in virtually any of the photos Tony and I have taken over the years. Yet they seem like they know me, like I'm an active part of their definition of the family.

I don't know them at all, and I want to remedy that. I've lost so many loved ones in recent years. On my mother's side, I've lost my great-aunts Rebecca and Alean, my great-uncle Big Baby, and most recently, my grandfather. On my father's side, my great-grandmother Marion Washington, my great-aunt Annette, and her husband, Joe, have all passed on. Not only were they souls I knew and loved but, more importantly, I assumed they would always be there. I never considered that I would see them die. I never thought the day would come when photo and video would be all that remained of them on this plane.

So now, even though these men are new to me, even though they feel like strangers, I need to bring them into the familiar. I need to know them and their stories before they too cross over into the unknown. Thus, I push Record and start asking questions.

"I had to go to work," Bruh says of his reasons for coming to Norwalk from Greenville on June 1, 1961. "When I was in high school I used to come to Washington and work during the summer, but in Washington they worked on Saturday and Sunday, and me being a country boy I wasn't going for that. In Washington most of the work was in restaurants and hotels. That was the only thing that Black people could do back in them days. But up here there were factories where you mostly worked five days a week. That was the only thing to do because we came off the farm with no skills. I was just glad to get out of the cotton fields."

When I hear the words *cotton* and *field* together, I think of slavery and sharecropping and the things that I envision as being so far removed from me that they exist only in history books. I don't make the connection that it takes normal, average, unknown people to create that thing we call history. And Bruh remembers the field life as if it were yesterday, as if the Greenville house where he and his brothers grew up were still standing and not just marked by the aproned driveway where they used to play before dinner. Bruh is one of the last living Langleys to have truly lived that old-school existence of rising at the rooster's crow to work on the farm, falling into bed, and having time in between only for meals and the Lord.

"It was pretty much over with by the time my brothers came along," Bruh says.

"It was over with when I stepped in the field," James Marvin jokes.

Agriculture didn't offer as much of a future as it had in the past, and at the time Greenville didn't have much else to offer its young. Bruh's sister Yvonne was the first to follow him to Norwalk but later moved to Dallas, Texas, where she married a military man. Ashley, Curtis, Douglas, and James Marvin came up later to finish high school, and upon graduating they too went to work alongside their eldest brother. Even now work keeps them together.

Five of the six of them went to work for Connecticut Light and Power, where Bruh became the first African American power lineman in the state. James took an early retirement and left the company in 1980 to form his own construction firm. But Bruh (still a lineman), Ashley (a meter reader), and Curtis (who works inside the city power plant) are still on the payroll.

"Coming here there were better jobs, more money, and a better chance for advancement," Bruh continues. "The jobs aren't as plentiful now. But there was a time here when you could quit one job, walk down the street, and get another one on the spot. In North Carolina, if you quit a job you might go six months before you found another one."

"Particularly if someone put the word out that they didn't like your work," Ashley adds. "Here you may not get in doing what you want. But you can always get a job to survive until you find what you want."

Work is for money. Money supports families, and families are things that never die. "We came here from North Carolina as a family and we stayed as a family. We've done so much for so long with so little it almost feels like you can do anything with nothing," James Marvin says about the Norwalk Langleys' solidarity over the last two generations.

But each man is very different. James Marvin is the most liberal of the bunch, while Ashley is the most conservative. At fifty-nine, Bruh, as the oldest, hovers above them all, giving off the status of an elder who has led his brethren to a promised land. So he always speaks first. Together they have added seven buds to their family tree, five men and two women, who now have their own children and live their own lives.

"You have to be a good worker," Ashley says about the values he's instilled in his twenty-one-year-old daughter Renee (not to be confused with Bruh's daughter of the same name). "No drugs. No alcohol. And you have to think before you speak. I taught her that if you speak first, you may say something that makes you look stupid, and once you say a word, a person will always remember what you say."

"You can lead a horse to water, but you can't make him drink," James Marvin adds about values. "The desire to do is something the kids have to have for themselves."

The brothers begin to chime in one after another, as if on cue, each defining his own individual space in the dialogue.

"You know many of the kids that were raised here today don't accomplish much," Ashley continues. "They're not used to working for the things that they get. They've never paid any rent, and when their parents die they're stranded and don't know what to do. Most of the kids our age who came up from the South who wanted to accomplish something accomplished quite a bit. Even if they didn't own property, they were willing and able to take care of themselves."

I sit there wondering what they think of me. I don't rise early to make a living. The only calluses on my hands come from banging on keyboards. Do they think I'm lazy? Spoiled? When I study their chiseled faces I imagine new definitions of struggle and perseverance, something far beyond eight hours at a desk and a crammed subway commute home. Yet they've lived their entire lives without smoking, drinking, or straying from the path their mother placed them on back in Greenville.

"It was almost zero tolerance for people my age," Bruh says about drugs and alcohol in Greenville. "I never saw a cigarette growing up. The only time I heard about drugs was when Jimi Hendrix died, and that hit me close to home because I was a Jimi Hendrix fan. Other generations seem to be able to tolerate it. But for me I'm still right where I started. I never moved."

"My mama used to tell us don't drink," James Marvin adds. "Falling all out in public was embarrassing. So we just thought it was the wrong thing to do. People didn't drink on the farm, and if they did it was only on the weekends."

"And when a farmer would drink he would only drink to get rid of his problems," Ashley continues, "when he couldn't pay his bills. But in the morning he'd be sober and ready to go back to workin' the fields, and the drinking didn't help him one bit."

These brothers don't talk about their father, even when I ask direct questions. At this point I make the mistake of assuming that he passed away early in their lives. But later I will discover a truth that is much different. I also know for a fact that my grandfather and his brothers didn't go through life completely clean and sober. And just as we experienced with my uncle Gary, addictions often destroyed those they loved. These things become more frighteningly clear when I finally sit down with Curtis's daughter Latanya sometime later.

As questions about morals and values continue, the subject switches to marriage. Both Bruh and James Marvin have been married twice, Ashley only once.

"It's not like it was thirty years ago," James Marvin says. "Thirty years ago if you had a wife you'd have that wife by your side no matter what."

Ann, James Marvin's second wife, sits at the table quietly, occasionally yelling over to the neighbors across the driveway. She offers us food, sodas, goes for ice cream at the corner, and answers the phone. But she doesn't contribute to the dialogue.

"I'm very old-fashioned," she says about the role she plays in her household. But when James Marvin asks who's in charge of the household, she grins and says, "Me."

"Years ago family came first," Bruh begins. "The man was the head of the house and whatever you said was basically what happened. Now with everybody working and everybody making their own decisions you got one person going one way and one person going the other. You don't know who's in charge anymore."

"When people first meet these days it's like buying a used car," Ashley says with a grain of disgust as the puffy clouds overhead begin to thicken and gray. "After they drive it awhile they just want another one."

"The problem with most marriages today is that people do not continue the way they started out," Bruh bellows. "Now when you're in love what the other person says is great, but when they get a little older it ain't great no more, so they don't want to do this no more and you can't do that. If you're not in it for the long haul then don't do it. The man should be the leader, and if you're gonna be the leader you can't get a girl pregnant and leave. That ain't leadin'. If you're a leader you have to take care of the family."

"My first wife was a city wife," James Marvin interrupts. "And they have different ideas about being married. They're not into flowers and gardens. When they get off work they want to go out and party. For a working man that's not on his menu. His menu is dinner on the table, the house cleaned, and that kind of stuff. When you start out they promise you every-thing under the sun and they make those promises to get out of those housing projects and places."

"My first wife wasn't bad," Bruh says reflectively. "But sometimes I pushed too much. I pushed myself real hard and I expected other people to work as hard and be as dedicated as I was. But as I got older I started to look at things differ-ently. If they don't want to go where I'm going, then fine. It's not about being a good or a bad person. You could be two good people but you can start to move in two opposite ways."

Bruh married Tina in 1986 and has three grandchildren from his children Gerald and Renee.

"We were taught to live by the Bible," James Marvin says as he reclines in his plastic seat, the bottom of his T-shirt rid-ing up to reveal a sliver of his globelike spare tire. "You're not necessarily gonna live one hundred percent by it, but you should live as close to one hundred percent as possible. Our rules were the Ten Commandments, and we felt like if you didn't violate all ten you couldn't be all bad."

The others look on as James Marvin continues. "In church, if you did something wrong, Mama used to just shake her head and you knew not to do it again. She took us to church every Sunday and every Bible study and every night they were studying something from the Bible. We had to watch every movie about the Bible that came on TV. And every night you had to watch the news at six and you had to be quiet." Their only nonreligious programming consisted of *Amos and Andy*, *Gunsmoke*, *Bonanza*, and *The Ed Sullivan Show*.

It's hard to sit there and listen to these men without re-sponding. From where I sit, so many of their views are so out-wardly chauvinistic and blind that I want to strap them to chairs, grill them, then force them to understand the error of their viewpoints.

Donnie, the youngest of the Norwalk Langleys, has stopped by to see me on his way to work. At forty-seven, he is the most prolific father of the bunch, with "six kids and no wife." He's dressed in a silk shirt and slacks, and I can picture him sipping Hennessey's at a bar before being a part of this clique.

"I could have brought the family, but there would have been more of them than you," he jokes. "It's not that I was wild or nuthin'," he says, referring to his large number of children. As an only child five kids seems pretty big to me. "It's just that I was always a straight shot," he adds.

Donnie also works for the power company, which merged into New York's Con Edison four years ago. He's the only person I actually remember from the reunion in the motel parking lot in Greenville years before.

Time passes and the conversation returns to work, the thing that aligns them all. At fifty-nine, forty-eight, and fifty-three, Bruh, James Marvin, and Ashley have begun to face the effects of technology on their occupational future. Ashley is a meter reader and has read meters at the homes of many celebrities, such as Martha Stewart, David Letterman, the late Rodney Dangerfield, and the late Luther Vandross.

But computerization will soon bring his job of thirty years to an end. Luckily for him he has seniority, so he'll get to drive a company van until he retires. Bruh, on the other hand, seems to be somewhat irreplaceable. With his thirty-eight years of experience, computers will have a hard time replacing him.

"It's kind of hard to replace me," he says. "They tried. But they can't find a computer that can tell you where every wire is or what it does. That just comes with years of experience."

"You'll never retire on a job for thirty years anymore," Donnie says matter-of-factly about the state of the blue-collar job market. "After four years and 364 days you're out of there."

"It's hard to say where it's going because it's all changing and changing fast," Bruh says about his view of the future. "The way I was brought up and the way I made it, you can't do that no more. Coming up with a high school education and making your way to the top on a job isn't going to happen. People aren't going to pay the money I make for a boy to come off the farm anymore."

The group also has very little faith in the current generation. They see people my age as spoiled and lazy children who don't want to do for themselves.

"You ask them if they want to go and see somewhere else and they tell you that they just want to stay and hang around here," James Marvin says. "We should give you a staff and let you lead them."

A figurative staff is placed within my grip by my grandfather's nephews. Even if we are strangers, we will always share blood. Their work and the work of their parents have made the way for my generation. We've finished high school. We've graduated from college. So many of us are able to afford the trappings of a comfortable life. Their work is coming to an end. Now it's our turn to step up to the plate.

Just then droplets from the sky drive the group into James Marvin's basement, where we are warmly greeted by a big-screen TV and a bar with liquor that hasn't been opened since their father was alive.

We speak about the mystery of the Lone Ranger, about

the man beneath the strong and silent subterfuge. I hear for the first time that Willie, Frank, and Jesse were only half-brothers, sharing a father in one Cecil Tyson. Willie and Frank were born to Lily-Anne Langley, daughter of Drew and William-Anne Langley (yes, that's a woman's name). The identity of Jesse's mother, however, is unknown to them.

I have written in fiction about motherless children, about how their lack of female nurturing can curse them with an inability to express themselves. Those characters feel awkward in matters of emotion and can express themselves only through silence or the rawest forms of anger. Is it just a coincidence that the model for such a child was so close to me? Or have I been telling Jesse Langley's story for longer than it has appeared?

The conversation continues to the subject of my parents' wedding. All six brothers came down to Bethesda Baptist Church on November 20, 1971, exactly four years before I was born. My mother arrived at the church in Ashley's gold Pontiac Grand Prix.

They called my mother's head wrap a turban and wondered why my father wore a dashiki instead of a suit. Bruh is particularly close to my mother, having spent time with her during his summers in DC as a teenager.

"She used to always talk so proper," he says with a grin. James Marvin shows me a photo of her. She looks youthful and extremely petite with a huge Afro, tight jeans, and an embroidered shirt. The Polaroid is faded and I can barely make out her face. But I know it's her. After all these years she still smiles the same way. And the world happily smiles along with her.

"One of the things that always bothered us was that Junie, Tony, and Gary don't seem to stick together like we do," Bruh says with concern.

He has a point: my uncles are three different men who have taken three different paths that practically never intersect. Sure there's Thanksgiving and Christmas and the Fourth, but they are far from spending their Sundays in a backyard talking about good times and bad, work and life. I come to understand that in a way we, as the DC arm of the clan, are the black sheep and not the other way around.

My uncles never hug each other. They rarely exchange phone calls other than when it has to do with Sally Helen or the family as a whole. They seem to have so little in common for boys so close in age.

The only things they seem to be able to expound on are their shared experiences in Trinidad and their father's house. And their perceptions of those experiences are radically different.

While Bruh and his crew all traveled to Norwalk with similar goals, the Lone Ranger's kin scattered. Tony chose the comfort of his mother and later settled in locales far away. Gary chose his father, the streets, and an addiction he couldn't kick. Junie for the longest time chose only himself.

But no matter how much tape rolls, I can't seem to get what I want about Jesse Langley, Sr. It doesn't all come together in some nice little bow like a feature for some fluff magazine. There are loose ends and unanswered questions, things that may never be explained. My great-grandmother is in a grave I'll never find. My uncles learned manhood from a patriarch who never really knew his own daddy. The answers have only provided more questions, and my journey is long from over. There has to be someone else who knows something that can fill in the blanks, someone closer to home, someone I still have yet to meet.

The rain has ended when we return to our respective cars.

James Marvin notices the slow leak in my tire and offers to give me some air. He uses a small pump connected by an exposed wire to a rechargable battery. I have to smile to myself. This is ghetto engineering at its best.

I promise everyone that I will return. Donnie promises seafood and I jokingly promise Donnie to bring a single woman for him. I hug them like the family they are and follow Ashley's Civic back to the interstate, smiling all the way, knowing that this is just the beginning.

2

Bed-Stuy pool legend "Slim" Parham once reminded me that the world cannot survive without conflict. If atoms didn't smash, if forests didn't burn, if evil didn't so often seem to outweigh good, then we'd be living in a world that was forever standing still.

I think of this as the perfect blue sky above is concealed by ashen gray, as thunder murmurs off in the distance. The dark clouds have to open if that rich color is ever to return. Especially when they are the last of an ordeal named "Ivan," the relentless force of nature that flooded the Richmond train station where I was supposed to arrive. My uncle Tony and Jerome, joined by my second cousin Cordelia, have instead scooped me from a secondary station just beyond the city limits.

A few hours later I am standing on the gravel path that separates the modular home of my great-aunt Mae Ross (widow of Sally Helen's youngest brother, Alfred Smith, aka Big Baby) from the decaying abode where she and her late husband raised five daughters to adulthood. Those little girls are long gone now. Each has become a woman out in the world with her own kids and grandkids to boot.

Yet the house itself still stands. Though the ivy and weeds have found their way through every crack and crevice, though the well of the cleanest water I've ever tasted has run dry, this landmark of things past is still erect. A few yards into the woods are the remains of an old wagon, one that was once drawn by horses and filled to the brim with hay—or was it corn, or tobacco, or something else altogether? There's also a toolshed, an old pickup with a cab swiss-cheesed by rust at the rear, and the frame for an old futon someone must have forgotten about, all strewn across the rear border of the property.

I remember being a boy out in the place, running through the woods and fields to catch everything from wicked mosquito bites to half a torso's worth of poison ivy. This is Powhatan, Sally Helen's home, the place where I spent a week of every year until I went off to college. This is the place where dogs would howl all through the night, where the cows mooed my city-boy behind into the morning.

Now, with Tony only a half hour away, I wanted to see the family. I wanted to see if and how things had changed. So many of the old faces have vanished, delivered either to the grave, nursing homes, or off to big cities for better jobs and the race to keep up with the Joneses. The pastor I remember at the family church, Mt. Pero Baptist, has been replaced multiple times. The latest incarnation wears the shame of having shorted Jerome on his fee for playing the piano during services.

The two-story house where my great-grandmother Lucy Smith died has been devoured by nature. It's no longer visible from the main drag once used to gain access. Even the dirt road has been swallowed up by weeds and foliage. It was the first place where I ever saw closed cocoons for morphing butterflies. The oak in the front yard had branches it took me nearly four years to learn how to climb. It was a place where I could hear dogs howling while I slept and roosters crowing early in the morning, my only connections to the life my mother's mother had once lived.

Now that life is lost, like those that have passed on, taken back by the elements. I miss them all, all the uncles, aunts, and cousins who bowed out long before I came through the birth canal, those who still speak to me from the next realm, whispering everything from their names and desires to who really won the 2000 election. But those stories are for another time.

I am snatched out of a trance as someone calls my name on this side. My third cousin LaToya asks me to help her marinate and flip burgers on the smoking grill just a few feet away. Jade, her two-year-old daughter, still eyes me with suspicion. After all, I am a new face, even if I have been around for the past three hours. Toya, twenty-nine, and her younger sisters Tiffany, twenty-four, and Michelle, twenty-two, never knew the inside of the old house with the old well at the back, or for that matter the bucolic life upon which I am reflecting.

Their grandmother Mae Ross's newer home is less than fifty yards from the old one. Within its yellow siding, the single-level three-bedroom residence houses a VCR, cable TV, indoor plumbing, and more copies of *Ebony* magazine than I can count. The rural life ain't so rural anymore.

Toya and Tiffany are both single mothers, or at least mothers with children not living with their baby-daddy's. They have their own cars and clothes that keep up with ever more hip-hop times. Thus there's a temporal divider between them and that building across the path.

They know what it was. They can even understand its significance to their family history. But it's got nothing to do with their day-to-day. The closest they've come to working the fields is fiddling with the reception on reruns of *Living Single*. But there are some still alive who can remember what life was like so long ago for Willie Langley and his brothers. And that reminds me of the woman I have just visited, a woman who thought her family's work on the farm would never end, that she'd spend the rest of her life watching those she loved suffer under the hand of oppressors posing as chairmen of the board.

She was the strange face behind the door I opened the night after my grandfather's passing. There she was, dressed in dark blue, her hair covered with a wig of synthetic brown twists. Being my usually protective (and often paranoid) self, I wanted to ask her who the hell she was and what she was doing showing up at my family's home just because someone had died. Where had she been for Sunday dinner? How come I had never seen her on Christmas or the holidays? Why didn't we share the smallest glimmer of recognition?

The truth was that she had been in Jesse Langley's life a lot longer than I had. The truth was that she had been one of the few folks in the Lone Ranger's life who knew him well.

A little fair-skinned sweetheart named Christine Worthington was the little girl the Lone Ranger came back to Greenville to visit every now and again as his family on Childress Street began to flourish. The daughter of Jesse's half-sister Mary (they shared a father in Cecil Tyson), she had no idea what a crucial role he would play in her life.

"When I first met Uncle Jesse I was in the seventh grade,"

she tells me from the dining room of the apartment she shares with her husband, Shannon, in New Carrollton, Maryland, just a hop, skip, and jump beyond the DC border.

"The first time he came to visit I didn't even know my mother had a brother," she says. "But he would come to Greenville from Washington, DC, from time to time."

One of nine children, she and her siblings were put to work in the Carolina fields as soon as they were able. They toiled in the hard heat six days a week and did without school for weeks at a time to help the family keep up with planting and harvesting. She can still remember seeing that school bus cruising by while she worked early each morning, its presence reminding her that others were having the chance to learn while she was giving her young spine the chance to ache.

"We farmed peanuts, cucumbers, soybeans, corn, tobacco, and anything else my father could put into the ground," she recalls. "Corn comes in those tall stalks. First you have to plant it and then you have to go back to harvest it. We'd have to take the ear in our hands and pull it off the stalk and then put it in piles, pick the piles up and put them in a wagon, and then take the wagon inside the barn to unload it."

Shucking corn is a far cry from mowing the lawn or doing the dishes or cleaning out the tub once a week. For her and her siblings, chores weren't meant to teach character or responsibility. They served a single purpose: to aid in the family's survival.

Her father, Johnny Harris, was a good man in his own way, she tells me, but he "carried an attitude" and would curse his kids out in a minute. According to her, his anger came from frustration, the frustration of never seeming to get anywhere. He'd work all year and come harvest time almost all the money would go to the farm's owner under the guise of the smash-and-grab system historians would describe as *share-cropping*—the business of working Black families like their enslaved ancestors for crumbs from the pie's crust.

Under such a system, Johnny, like more Black men than can ever be named, couldn't take care of his own in the way the Bible told him he should. Being uneducated and disenfranchised, he could do nothing about it.

"Back then you didn't talk back to the white man. You didn't give him a piece of your mind. But when I came up I did."

When she was thirteen, Christine realized that the owner, Dempsey Clark, was cheating her father. Clark would take the money the family was supposed to get and use it to pay *his* field hands, which meant that her father and his kin got nothing: no money or food or even a horse to ride out on. Though she missed school for weeks at a time, the girl always caught up when she returned to the classroom. And as it turned out, math was her best subject. So when her youthful eyes observed that the money wasn't coming in right, she felt obligated to speak her piece.

"I'd sit there every Friday, and the numbers wouldn't add up. So one day I went over and knocked on Mr. Clark's door and told him that I knew what he was doing. That we didn't have enough food, clothes, or anything."

For months, Clark stonewalled her by saying that he had to deal only with her father. But on one particular Saturday, young Christine, flanked by her older sister Minnie, came to Clark's door with exact figures in her hands. After that Clark had to come forth with a cleaner share, money her father used to allow her defiant daughter to finish school and graduate. Unfortunately Johnny never saw her cross that stage and get her diploma. He died at age fifty-three on October 2, 1962, seven months before her graduation on May 31, 1963, at Bethany High School in Bethel, North Carolina.

I imagine the country breeze of the Cackalacs to be little different from that of Powhatan, Virginia. Like Sally Helen, Christine knew her future was elsewhere. The question was where she would go to find it. With no money for college and the job prospects in her neck of the woods limited to house-wife and . . . housewife, she had to blaze her own trail. So in 1964 she left Greenville to live with her sister Minnie and Minnie's husband in Danbury, Connecticut.

"Minnie used to go to church all the time," she remem-bers. "And I remember one Sunday this preacher came up from Durham, North Carolina, named Inez Choke. And she was preaching about God as 'Mr. Wonderful.' After I listened to her, I knew that I didn't have Mr. Wonderful, and I needed him to take me through life, so I accepted Christ."

As they say before they dunk you in the water, she was "made anew." Through Jesus Christ her savior, she was born again.

"I would have dreams where I would see the word of God written across the skies. God told me to tell my brothers and sisters that the wages of sin is death and the gift of God is eter-nal life. But I didn't want to preach. I ran from it for many years. I told God that it wasn't a job for me. But by 1969, when I came to DC, I knew that God had called me to the ministry."

Christine rolled into Chocolate City at twenty-two with nothing but a suitcase and her uncle Jesse's phone number. She needed a job but didn't have any major leads. By chance she found a posting for some position in a local paper. But since Jesse delivered milk to so many different places, he had inside job sources all over. She couldn't even inquire about the one lead she'd found before her mother's brother told her that a company called GSA needed a cook.

"When I went in the interviewer thought Uncle Jesse was my husband. So when we were in there he helped me show the guy how much personality I had just by being himself." Jesse made little jokes and told her to let the man know about all the things she'd done in her life. All she wanted was for the guy to say that she was hired, but because of her good uncle's finesse she walked out as the place's new cashier instead of landing the lower-paying cook's post she'd come there for.

Jesse was there for her wedding to Shannon Cooley and came by soon after the birth of their son, Jeffrey. They talked often about the Bible and the folks back at home. As the years passed, the number of those "folks" continued to dwindle, until only two in the handful remained. Even I can remember his lamentations on the subject, the lonely days he'd spend out on that porch after learning that someone else had passed on, that the Lord was keeping him here while so many others got to go home. Perhaps there was something about that displacement that made him a little mischievous because, according to Christine, the Lone Ranger liked to create his own kind of drama.

Once upon a time the two were supposed to drive down to Greenville together. But when it was time to leave, Christine, in Jesse's opinion, was taking too long. So without so much as a word he took a bus from Greenville back to Childress Street, leaving Christine to make the six-hour drive on her own. When she got back, she headed straight to his house to confront him only to find out that she'd beat his bus there.

"And he had the nerve to tell me that he took the bus because I was too slow," she laughs. "We had a little falling out over that, but we ended up laughing about it. Because there were so many times he came to me and my children's rescue. He gave me money when my mother died and I had to go back to Greenville to get my son and my niece Alice, whom I had both raised. When Minnie and her husband had an argument, I'd go and get Uncle Jesse. If I would see Gary in trouble with the police, I would call Uncle Jesse. We just had a really tight relationship."

Older than his own children, Christine was Jesse's DC key to the life he'd left behind. In her he could see his sister Mary, the soul filled with fire that he had loved to clash with as a younger man.

"He'd call me up and want to make me argue with him, in just the way my mother used to put him in his place," she remembers. "And he enjoyed that. The reason I know that is because he called my sister one night and told her that he had tried to get me to argue with him and I wouldn't. He wanted to keep the aggressiveness my mother had alive in me so that when she died he'd have someone else to argue with."

He would tease her by saying, "You don't love me. You talk love. See, God's people love with their heart and you only love with your lips." Then he'd say that her other sisters loved him more than she did, just to get her "real fired up." And once she was ablaze he'd come in with the cooling "I know you love me."

When she finally gave in to her calling and became a minister, he'd dial her number and say, "Hello Holy Ghost." Or he'd finish reading a passage from the Bible and call her up to argue about its meaning, just to keep the drama going.

In July of 1990, when Christine climbed before a congregation to preach her first sermon, the Lone Ranger was there.

"He said, 'Wow, you preached better than my preacher!' "

she recalls. "But even though he fell in love with my preaching, he would always say that a woman is not called to preach. In his mind there were so many things women weren't supposed to do. In my case it was women didn't have no business preachin'."

I imagine Christine as the counterpart my grandfather needed in a life spent with Sally Helen. Christine was more like him, someone who knew only work and the ways of the Lord. I don't read her as the type to open her arms wide and hug the world or to make a full meal upon the arrival of perfect strangers. Her home screams of someone who understands struggle. The framed portrait of Frederick Douglass and the figurines of the buffalo soldiers are indicative of a mind that understands that each African American is part of a community that is at war, battling against poverty, racism, and most important, against Satan himself.

"This current generation's attitudes are so different from the ones we had when we were coming up," she declares. "We were taught respect and we implemented respect. They're more aggressive about getting what they want, but they're also far more violent." To her the state of the Black community is a product of the last two generations' lack of discipline.

"The Bible says to 'spoil not the world, because if you spoil the world you spoil a child,' " she continues. "We're not able to discipline our children the way we were disciplined. Because now if you hit your children someone might call the police on you and you're sent to jail. In our time it was child abuse but we didn't know it. I can remember some of those whippings even now. When you did something back then your parents didn't forget it. They didn't threaten you with a whipping and not deliver it. And in that way the government has now hindered the proper disciplining of our children."

More important, she sees the influx of illegal immigrants as the greatest threat to African American survival. Shannon, her husband, has been a member in his labor union for ten years and still can't find work when he's competing with those who will work longer hours for less.

"We've been put on the back burner," she says. "After all these years the Black man is still looking for a way to support his family."

She herself hasn't worked since 1972 due to a back injury. But she is "doing the work of God" with a good husband and beautiful children. And the Lord always makes a way.

"I am a true believer in God and his miraculous power," she says, "and I'm not afraid to stand toe to toe with the devil."

"What is it?" Toya asks me as I come toward her. I am staring at the old well, remembering the excitement I felt the first time Mae Ross drew water from it. It was like *Little House on the Prairie* made real. Now the well is old and dry, drained of its life-giving waters by time. All things end so that others can begin. Sally Helen's children are becoming the elders and I am becoming a man.

The burgers have been marinated in honey and barbecue sauce, accented with red pepper and some cumin, a combination I am particularly proud of. Combined with the smell of the grill, I am reminded of all that I long for when I'm in Brooklyn.

I look into Toya's big round eyes and for some reason see Christine. Toya too is a mother and a fighter and a woman far from being down with the "okie doke" many of her peers succumb to. She asks me about New York, and sometimes about the world as a whole. What remains of this dying town isn't enough to hold her or her younger siblings. Maybe soon she will venture out beyond her borders. And maybe I'll be her Uncle Jesse, making sure she gets there.

The silence is broken by Jade, who says my name as if the *i* were short. For a beat I think of my own child, of the blending of myself and another within a womb. The image pulls at something deep within me and does not let go.

"Nothing," I say to Toya's question. "Those burgers ready yet?"

3

Greenville is gone. Or at least the one the Lone Ranger knew. When he left to seek his fortune in the nation's capital, his hometown offered only two career paths. You could work at the local cigarette packaging plant or in the fields. Nowadays corporate America runs the place. Kaiser Permanente and Kelly-Springfield have moved in, as have medical schools and universities. Someone growing up here now just might have a future.

However, I am not standing in Greenville. The Langley house and farm, like those who inhabited it, are long gone. For this story it is now just a place on a map, much like ancient Kemet in comparison to Egypt, which is now considered another part of the Middle East.

I am more than a hundred miles to the northwest in Fayetteville, North Carolina, in search of yet another person who can give me answers, someone who remembers Jesse Langley, Sr., as the young man setting out to seek his fortune.

She is a woman who for the sake of her privacy does not want to be named, but whose relation to the man in question defines her vividly enough.

It's Halloween 2004 and all the kiddies are gathering in their costumes for the night's candy run. They are dressed as Jedis and SpongeBob Squarepants, as witches and monsters and the ever-popular white-sheet-with-eyes-cut-out ghosts, their empty shopping bags ready to be filled beneath foliage that has turned nearly every color imaginable. It's the kind of autumn I miss in New York, the kind that reminds me of how few trees there are outside of the parks in the Rotten Apple's most dangerous borough.

My source (let's call her Daphne) has lived in the house I'm visiting since her only daughter, whom we'll call Paula, was born. Paula is now a dean of students at a prestigious university and a well-paid researcher for the U.S. Department of Education. Daphne moved here in 1960 and began a forty-five-plus year career as a teacher, one that continues to this very day.

Daphne is the eldest child of Willie and Hattie Langley, and one of the eight boys and girls who were coming into the world as the Lone Ranger made his escape from the only town he knew. She's the only one of those eight who still lives in the state of North Carolina. Her brothers are in Norwalk, and her younger sister Yvonne is out in Dallas. She was only a little girl when the Lone Ranger took leave of the only town he had ever known, which, according to her, was very uncharacteristic for people at the time.

"His generation was kind of slow to explore beyond their immediate surroundings," Daphne begins. "I think it was out of fear. They didn't leave because they were afraid of what was beyond."

Jesse, however, was not afraid. He had very little to lose by leaving. Having never known his father, Cecil, or his mother, he, along with his brothers Willie and Frank, was reared by his grandparents, "Daddy" Drew Langley and his wife William-Anne. That so-called rearing was less about hugs and kisses and more about getting the jobs done that needed to get done to keep a farming family alive. He, Willie, and Frank all but raised themselves, with Jesse as youngest brother surprisingly having to be the most self-sufficient.

But boys cannot fill the shoes of men. The Langley brothers' manhood was not formed from the most thorough of molds and was thus incomplete. Daphne saw this most clearly through living with (or living through, depending on how you view it) her father. Willie was apparently the biggest handful of the three.

"I couldn't define him as being a father," she says of Willie. "Maybe he didn't know how to be [one]. Maybe he did the best he could. But I don't know about that. I know my mother did the best she could with eight children. I, as the oldest, had to take on the responsibility when things weren't going right. With those experiences I knew what *not* to do as a parent."

She witnessed her father doing some ugly things in her formative years. There was alcoholism, spousal abuse of the physical and verbal varieties, and he seemed to have a real lack of love for everyone around him. As the eldest, it was her job to blaze the trail that her other siblings would follow. So she made a serious decision at seventeen. She was going to make it, no matter what.

"I was determined that wherever I went I would move on, that I would be successful no matter what," she says. "I would not work for minimum wage or live anywhere where I'd have to pinch pennies. That meant doing more than moving from one side of town to the other like most people did. I'd seen so many people sabotaged by fear."

She vividly remembers a conversation she had with her uncle Frank just after her high school graduation. He asked her what she planned to do next. She told him that she wanted to go to college.

She continues, "And he said, 'Well, you've graduated from high school. What is it you want to learn now? Why are you trying to go to college? No one else in this family has ever gone.' I told him that maybe that was by choice, but that I would be going. He asked me who was going to pay for it since my daddy couldn't. And I told him I'd get to that when I got to it.

"Those kinds of things let me know as I got older that there was so much insecurity in them. Just like what slave masters did to slaves. Kept them scared so they couldn't function. Get some to tell on each other. Some Blacks still do that today, pit each other against one another so we won't be successful."

She was not alone in her decision to leave. Most of the kids in Greenville who graduated between 1956 and 1965 got out of Dodge as soon as diplomas were in hand. There had to be more to life than working at the cigarette plant or pulling crops out of the ground. It was also the '60s. The movement was sweeping through the South.

"We'd get the white folks to march with us because they also wanted us to have our civil rights," she remembers, "and we'd march with them because they wanted to burn their bras and save the birds and all of that other stuff."

Change was in the air. Those kids off the farm wanted more, and Daphne was just as hungry as the rest of them.

While she went to the University of North Carolina (she found the money somewhere), her friends attended North Carolina A&T and Hampton, Virginia State, Howard, and Johnson C. Smith in Charlotte. If they didn't go to school, they went to work, like her younger brothers did up in Connecticut. Her sister Yvonne married a military man and spent twenty-two years following him wherever he went. Daphne, perhaps the most progressive of all eight, ended up closest to home after she married a man whose name she doesn't even mention. She hasn't remarried since.

Teaching is her business, and she does it well. Certified for kindergarten through the sixth grade, she's currently in another arena altogether: music. Her school system was short on music teachers so they called her back from the brink of her retirement to lend a hand. Being an excellent pianist turned out to be a big plus. She can't say how much longer she'll continue, only that she'll evaluate how she feels at the end of each year. This is not the same school system she started out in. More important, these are not the same kind of students she knew forty-five years ago.

"When I first started to teach, the children were more disciplined," she remarks. "They didn't have as much as they have now in the way of material things, but there was more parental support. So you could cover more in the way of learning. I have seen in the past ten or fifteen years the lack of parenting. Parents are not as interested in the school. They don't come as much or want to volunteer and be involved. I read some stats that said forty percent of all beginning teachers leave the profession within the first five years. So that tells you how demanding it is."

A lot of her kids are growing up living with grandparents and great-grandparents who have their own children while their parents are in the armed forces. Fayetteville is a military town with one army and two air force bases. So many moms and a few dads are overseas.

"And it's a shame because Black children are often discounted and written off because it's thought they can't do certain things," she says. "That's one of my pet peeves. I tell my students all the time that they should never ever let anyone tell them what they're capable of doing, because they don't know."

Listening to her I think of my mother, of how little was left of her after class was dismissed, her tote bag stuffed with papers to be graded, lists of parents to be called, many of whom never appreciated the effort.

Then I think of the teenaged boys I teach in an after-school program in Bed-Stuy, young men who swear to God they know everything in the world, that the best life has to offer is a six-figure sports car with chrome rims and the latest in designer clothing. A teacher's life in this country has only become more difficult with fewer rewards. Women like Mom and Daphne are my heroes, because I know I'd barely last a year teaching in a public school system, much less the thirty-plus both of them have served.

"I got married after I'd taught ten years," she says. "I said if it works and it looks good I'll be in it. If it wasn't I'll be out. After eleven months I was out. I had moved up to New Jersey with him but I came back to Fayetteville and got a job with the same school system I'd left."

I have to mention that she left her husband while she was pregnant.

"Yvonne stayed with her husband twenty years. But I didn't stay twenty months," she says. "I guess I'm a visionary. I saw that things weren't going to be what I thought should be a healthy relationship. I don't believe in making things work. I think they should just work, if everything is healthy. So I removed myself because I wasn't happy. Paula was born here. I would've left whether I was pregnant or not. There were no ifs, ands, or buts about it."

She had a baby one year, built her house the next year, and then proceeded to teach in the public schools five days a week, in a community college three nights a week, and then still taught piano and organ on Saturdays. She's sixty-six years old and still going at it. She's preparing pamphlets for an upcoming school open house as we speak.

Daphne's memories of the Lone Ranger are bittersweet, just like her reflections on Greenville—as a place of beauty with too many ugly memories, a world to remember fondly but to stay the hell away from. She can recall Jesse's visits to Willie and Hattie's home when she was a little girl, and how he'd always say he wanted young Daphne to come up and visit as her uncle Frank and great-grandmother William-Anne had. He seemed like he was doing all right up there, better than he ever could have if he had stayed in the place where he was born.

"He worked hard," she remembers. "He always worked hard. He told me he stood in line all day to get that job at the Wakefield Dairy (the other dairy Jesse worked at) and was about to give up right when he got hired. But I didn't think he was ever as happy as he should have been. He, my father, and Frank didn't enjoy life the way they should have because they didn't seek out the most positive things they could have. Self-pity can take that from you. I would tell him that when he made negative statements about people without knowing whether or not they were true. But he'd just blow me off. My dad used to do the same thing."

So much of how the Langley men turned out had to do with the when and where of their very existence.

"There was a climate back there then when they'd just complain a lot because they didn't know how to fix things," she continues. "Given the time, they had managed to survive despite all of the obstacles they faced. But I don't think Uncle Jesse was a very happy person. I think he had a lot of anger from his childhood. I think that manifested itself in all three of them.

"But they shouldn't have let it sabotage their being. You can't change anything bad that happened to you. You can't blame anyone else other than the person who might have caused it. He let those things bother him for years and years."

It's moments like these when I understand the saying that Black folks don't believe in psychotherapy. What doesn't kill you makes you stronger. Get the ball into the end zone and win the game. Only worry about your knees and spine on the mornings when you can't get out of bed because of the swelling.

Translation: There was no room for the Lone Ranger to have feelings about what he saw, about being orphaned, about not knowing how to form friendships, about failing to express his emotions to those he loved most. So he carried it all with him, cramming it all into a tiny room at the rear of his mind and welding the door shut.

What difference did his background make? He brought money home. His children were healthy and had a roof over their heads. Anything beyond that was superfluous, that is, until he no longer had a full house to provide for.

Perhaps my grandfather remained on that porch, and in his bedroom, and in his cab, and at that little table in the kitchen because those were the only places where he knew how to deal. There he could exist in silence without speaking, without running the risk that that door in the back of his mind might come undone, that there might be tears, or warm sticky confessions he never felt safe enough to utter.

And when he could not suppress this stuff, there were always the bottle and that pack of Lucky Strikes, the escape route that so many of us brothers choose because it's the easiest, the most accessible, the path of least resistance.

The implications race through my mind as if there's a prize at the end. How hard was it for him to watch Sally Helen effortlessly deal with people socially when he wasn't sure how to? How could he talk to his children about anything when no one had ever talked to him on topics besides God and the job? Were the precious moments when he smiled and joked and held his family in his arms the times when the man he wanted to be finally showed through?

As I sit there in Fayetteville, across from a relative stranger who feels familiar, there are more and more thoughts and nothing but dead air. Perhaps my grandfather chose to impart what he could of his true feelings to me because I didn't have a frame of reference. I didn't know him beyond the few years I'd spent in his world. I couldn't judge him because I didn't know where he'd been. Thus I was the only one who could do this, the only one who could tell this tale.

Just then I am flushed with an unfamiliar feeling, an invisible touch at the base of my skull. Once again it is the hand of my ancestors, their collective power informing me that I've finally found what I was looking for.

Daphne, her daughter, and her niece Latanya (Curtis's daughter) were key players in 1999's Langley family reunion up in Norwalk. Everyone was there except for Gary and me. Boy did I miss out. In the time that has followed all have regaled me with tales of how much fun it was: music and laughs and reflections on good times long gone. I am told that Bruh and his brothers, along with Junie, Jay, my mother, and Sally Helen, all cut a rug in the rented space. They danced to songs old and new and ate until they were completely stuffed two nights over.

There was no real schedule for the festivities, nor any detailed synopsis of the goings-on that I can describe for you like the lyrics of the Jill Scott track. It was just a weekend of family being together, of different people from different places finding common ground in the name of the blood they all shared.

Thus, I know that the Lone Ranger was there among them, happy that he'd paved the way for those he loved to enjoy themselves. He would've sat in a corner with his plate and watched, saying very little and doing even less, but still playing his part. In his mind he didn't have to speak to be heard. He didn't have to move to make things happen.

"You set the course for your children and they will not go wrong," Daphne says in closing, sounding like a verse from the Good Book. "But you have to provide for them emotional as well as financial support."

You have to have both. That's probably the most important thing Jesse and his brothers never got to learn. You have to have both.

4

I've stood at this gate more times than I could possibly remember. There was a time when the iron handle and thumb latch seemed almost as high as heaven. But soon they reached down to eye level, then to my shoulder. Next thing I knew, I could swing the gate open as easily as my father had on the many nights he carried me in.

The basement apartment of 3807 W Street SE had more than its share of problems in the eighteen years I lived there. In a building-length condo on the lowest floor, we inherited all the sins of our fellow tenants. Bad pipes brought water damage to our carpet and ceilings every other year. It was hard to sleep because I could always hear people walking outside our gate toward other buildings. There were dustups with roaches and even a few with mice. But it was home to me, the last place my parents shared together, the only set of walls and rooms that remind me of the few years when things seemed complete.

Whoever came up with the idea for the Fairfax Village development had a pretty good concept. Build apartments and town houses together for lower- and middle-class folks and you'll have yourself a nice little community. Plenty of grass and trees on the other side of the road from Hillcrest, the city's southeastern haven for upper-middle-class African Americans.

It was so unlike anything my parents had known, far more spacious and free than what they'd had in Trinidad, a place where their little boy could grow without worry, a place where he would be safe from all that they'd endured. I loved to feel the wind against my face as I cruised down Thirty-eighth Street on my red Western Flyer with the BMX handle-bars. Butchie and I swung as high as we could on the Village playground swings before climbing the story-high sets of garages, only to scale down the pine tree at the far end of them.

I never knew what a ghetto was. As a matter of fact, the first time I ever heard the term was on an episode of *Good Times*. The terrain I knew was quiet and friendly. All the neighbors knew each other, from the Wormingtons to the Glymphs, to the Cunninghams and Texeras up the street. Everything was in perfect harmony.

But things started to change as the '80s came to an end. The Village began to attract a new element. A building just beyond the development became Section 8 housing. The low-income cribs known as the Continental Apartments started to get a little rowdy. Four twelve-year-old boys came up to our playground and beat a kid named Kenneth Middleton with metal bats before firing about twenty metal BBs into his chest. I can still see all the bloody holes, each filled with a tiny pool of crimson.

Wars started between us and various "them." Just because I was too small to take my place in battle didn't mean that I didn't see how serious it all was. The next thing I knew, mu-sicians were shouting out "FFC" (Fairfax Crew) on go-go concert tapes, indicating that we were on the map, that "the Village" was a place you didn't go without an invitation.

Thieves robbed our home on three different occasions. With the last burglary, I barely missed them, arriving only minutes after they'd left. I found my dog locked in a room and my refrigerator wide open. Joe would've taken the hand off of anyone he didn't trust. Those last burglars were people I knew.

Homeboys died and others went to jail. Girls got pregnant

and others moved away. By the time I was seventeen, Chocolate City had a minimum of two murders a night, the victims
usually under twenty-one. The Pope Funeral Home on Pennsylvania Avenue seemed to be open 24/7 and the cops were
switching from .38s to Glocks and 12-gauges.

All of this was popping off just as gangsters were sinking
their claws into hip-hop culture. Groups like the Native
Tongues Posse and Public Enemy were sharing space with
NWA, Ice-T, and Kool G. Rap. Their music and imagery reminded us all that we had to be hard out in our streets, even
if our streets required no such outlook. Treach, lead rapper of
the group Naughty By Nature, became spokesman for the attitude that personified the period on "Ghetto Bastard":

> *If you ain't never been to the ghetto*
> *Don't come to the ghetto*
> *'cuz you wouldn't understand the ghetto*
> *so stay the fuck out of the ghetto.*

Our neighborhoods, no matter how poor or rich, no matter how ugly or picturesque, became our ghettos, places we
proudly believed to be the only ones where we belonged,
even if our parents had wanted so much better for us, even if
they'd worked hard so that we could go anywhere we wanted.
If you weren't "ghetto," if you didn't represent your hood by
fighting for it at some party or getting some girl with the
right kind of ass, or if you weren't willing to die for it at the
hands of another crew's clip, then you weren't real, you
weren't down.

I never had any illusions about my own street credibility. I
knew who I knew, had fought who I had fought, and got
jumped by whoever caught me slipping at the given place and

time. I didn't represent anything other than myself. And even when I wanted to back my boys up, the Creator always had it that I was somewhere else, or sick, or otherwise unavailable when the given beef went down. I wanted more out of life than what the hood had to offer. I wanted to see the world, and that's where my path seemed to be leading me.

My grandfather had the same impulse when he said goodbye to Greenville. His expedition took him north. I went south. DC brought him a home, a wife, and a family. Atlanta brought me an understanding that I was not alone in what I chose and desired. Beyond DC's limits I was no longer relegated to a given position, no longer crippled by my creativity and academic achievement.

Beyond home the insults of my peers could never be as piercing. I could be anything I wanted to be without open critique. I could wear colors beyond the uniform black and gray T-shirts and sweatpants. I could grow my hair into locks without ridicule. And I could put my city into perspective, comparing it with the rest of the world full of Black people I'd read about.

At Morehouse I would spend many a freshman year night standing in the hallway with my dorm mates talking about fallen friends and urban decay. We were all the one guy who'd had enough, the one person who saw beyond the bullshit. We'd all come to this school to make our dreams come true, and to show the people we'd left behind that there were other ways out of the neighborhood beyond record deals and athletic scholarships.

From those talks we learned about towns we'd never been to and heroes we'd never read about. We listened to regional music we'd never heard before and borrowed things from each other's style and dress. We grew and kept growing.

But at the end of each school year we came home to the hood. We embraced our friends and family but often found that while we had done so much changing, so many others had remained the same. While we were learning, they were still grinding it out, still loitering on corners to holler at increasingly underage girls, still working retail and blowing all their dough on weed and car notes they couldn't afford. Some had made a life for themselves, but most were barely making it, even when they were living in houses that their parents owned and driving with insurance they didn't pay for.

I imagine that Jesse Langley, Sr., came home to much of the same. Daddy Drew had died when Jesse was barely a man and William-Anne passed just as Daphne finished high school. More and more of the faces he knew diminished until Greenville became nothing but an echo of its former self. As with my father, it became more and more difficult for Jesse to go home, because the home he knew was disappearing, and that was just too painful.

So Jesse tried his best to help out his brothers. Both Willie and Frank shared his roof for a time, but both, being as displaced as he was, didn't feel like they belonged anywhere. He visited nieces and nephews in an attempt to see his own future, to bear witness to all that remained of the dying culture they'd all left behind in the name of progress. But in the end, what he found was that he was completely alone in his position: a Lone Ranger.

I haven't lived in my hometown since a three-month stretch in '98. But whenever I'm in the area, I try to go home. I pull up to the rear of 3807 W Street SE and walk up to the gate that used to be mine. Someone else lives there now.

The new tenants have lost the iron *A* that finished out the address on the fence and replaced it with a laminated decal.

They've repainted the iron bars we had installed after that last burglary, bars designed and installed by my church deacon, Frank Morton, who has since passed on. Joe is still buried in the yard, with his leash and the mat he used to sleep on at the foot of my bed. And I bet there's still glue on the back of the door in what used to be my bedroom, a remnant of a weekend self-commissioned art project I can barely remember.

This is not home for me anymore, even though I want it to be. All the people who made it home are gone and have been rebirthed ten times since. It's just a place. All that made it home is inside of me.

But like Sally and Jesse, Christine, Daphne, and the Norwalk boys, I and those like me are the exception and not the rule. So many in our communities never leave. They never explore. They never try anything else, either because they're afraid, or because they don't know anything else.

On a subway trip to Harlem, one of my students, a Brooklyn resident since birth, blurted out that he'd never been in Manhattan, that he'd have to tell his mother just how far away from home he'd gotten. For him a twenty-minute train ride was an expedition into foreign territory, something to be feared more than appreciated.

It appears that our situation has looped itself, that the failures of our parents have taken us back to the Lone Ranger's age, where people thought it was safer to stay where you were. It's safer to take what's given to you and aspire to nothing more. It's safer to complain and be trapped in a system than it is to engage it head-on. We've become prisoners of our fear and ignorance, victims of a more covert version of the same treatment our slave masters imposed upon us generations before, and we're allowing it to happen each and every time we refuse to empower ourselves.

Ever since I could walk, my parents were taking me places. I knew how to ride the subways by the time I was eight. I knew which bus could take me to any part of town I needed to go. I even knew the quiet places where no one could bother me. I've yet to see the Eiffel Tower, the Great Pyramids, or the Great Wall of China, but I know they are there, that it is worth the time and effort to experience them.

I know these things because Melvin and Angela made them clear to me. My parents provided me with all the tools I needed to know the world, with all the things that spark curiosity, the things that bring about questions and their answers and subsequently understanding. I thought every kid in the world was given this same set of tools, this same structured rearing meant to make us the best we could be. Yet the painful truth is almost the complete opposite.

I won't allow my child's choices to be limited to the neighborhood where he lays his head. I don't want her career choices to be based on those of characters on UPN sitcoms. I don't want any boy of mine to believe that the image of manhood is a heavily greased 50 Cent at the climax of a music video. Nor will I ever allow my daughter to believe that her body is her greatest or only asset.

My grandfather didn't want his children to be limited to a life in the fields and factories. He didn't want them ever to struggle or be at the mercy of white men. He didn't want their cars ever to stall or their cupboards ever to be bare. So he walked away from all he knew in search of something better.

Like him I can only do the best that I can. I can offer my child all my knowledge and resources, all my time, energy, and perspective. But there will still be things I'll miss. I will still have failures. I will still make mistakes. This human being I've helped to create will not be perfect, because none of us are.

The plan had been for Jesse Langley to show me his old home, for me to set foot on the soil he once worked with his own hands. Fate, however, was not on my side. What I can do is bring my kid to this place, to this block where its daddy's life began, and tell him or her of all the changes that have taken place since, and do the same with the building on Simms Place and the home Jesse Langley made on Childress Street, the place where so many of the stories I've described here came into being.

Upon returning to Brooklyn, I whisper these things into my woman's ever-expanding womb, hoping that they will be heard and felt, if not fully comprehended by my flesh and blood to be. I am the next link in the Lone Ranger's chain. I am a young man looking for a clear path to find the place that will be our home.

elder

1

Summer is beginning its descent
into fall. The blindingly white sky
outside is beginning to lose its lus-
ter as the hidden sun falls beneath
the horizon. My mother's living
room is quaint and cozy. In recent
months she's been doing renovations: new carpet, furniture, and a
brand-new bathroom upstairs that
features a ceiling light with about
twenty different functions. This
place, where I sit toward the end of
my Lone Ranger vision quest, is
supposed to be for guests only. I
have only been excused because
company's on the way.

My cousin Jeanette is on the
way over for our interview. At
thirty, she is a mother of three and
guardian for her teenaged half-
brother Tristan. She has lived in almost every corner of the nation's
capital, often surviving by nothing
but the grace of God. I have more
fingers than the times we've met,

the last being at our grandfather's funeral. We sat together in the front row with everyone else, though someone omitted her name from the list of surviving kin.

It shouldn't have been a shock when I learned that Gary had a daughter, a girl about my age. If it had been Junie I wouldn't have been surprised. With Tony it was out of the question. But with Gary, because of his addiction, because he'd never lived away from his parents' home, because I seldom saw him walking hand in hand with some designated girlfriend, I wasn't sure of what to think.

I'd spent the first twelve years of my life as Sally Helen and Jesse's only grandchild, cursed to explore the family home alone. I'd always wanted someone to go through all the drawers with, or to try on the hats and shoes that were way too big for me. Had that someone been there I might not have almost suffocated to death when I sealed myself into a portable wardrobe and then knocked it over, sealing its only open airway.

So I didn't know what to think when I cruised into the house one Christmas to find a strange woman sitting at the dining room table, her eyes struggling to make contact with the familiar and not familiar faces all around her. Sally Helen and my mother and Tony treated her as if she'd been there all along, as if selective amnesia had rendered her a UFO only to myself. Upon seeing her I offered a polite but cold "hello" and then slithered back into the kitchen to get the skinny from my mama.

"That's Jeanette," she said casually, while loading greens into a serving bowl. "That's Gary's daughter." Gary at that exact moment happened to be in the area. So being my father's child I just had to say something.

"So when did this happen?" I asked. A moment later I

wished that I wasn't such a smart-ass. He froze like a deer in headlights and dropped his head, as if I'd just called him out for wearing shoes with holes in the bottoms. He could give me nothing but a shrug of the shoulders before retreating to his room upstairs, the one next to the Lone Ranger's. Each of them had a place to hide.

I went back into the dining room and sat down across from my cousin, still trying to calculate how all of this had happened without my being aware. Mom hadn't mentioned it in our Sunday phone calls. Grandma hadn't brought it up either. Jeanette was twenty-six years old, which meant she could have been with us every Sunday, even for the full fifty-two of them that happened before I was born. And she would have, had it been up to her.

She arrives at my mom's place with a hug and a big smile, yelling up to my mother, who is unfortunately fast asleep (even though it's barely 9 p.m.) and then takes a seat before the microphone in my mom's spanking new chair. She's been waiting to do this for a long time.

"On my eighteenth birthday I asked my mother, 'Mom, why do I have a gap in my teeth?' " Jeanette begins. She tells me she had also wondered why she was taller than her mother with a larger shoe size. These were not traits that came from her mother, or the guy she thought was her daddy, a man who'd been behind bars ever since she was born. (She has requested that both their names be withheld.)

"But I never had any idea that she was going to tell me the man I thought was my father was not," she continues. "But I always knew Gary. My mother used to bring me over to the house to see him and Sally-Mom. So I thought he was my godfather."

We take a moment to laugh at how strange it is that we

never met, that in more than twenty years we can't recall even being in the same room.

"And if you did see me you weren't going to be like 'Oh that's my cousin.' You'd probably be like, 'Oh that's some girl.' " She's probably right.

As she was growing up, the Langleys were something she couldn't escape. When she was fourteen, the mayor's Summer Youth Employment Program gave her a position at Webb Elementary, barely two hundred yards from 1341 Childress. She stopped by the house every other day that summer. "Sally-Mom" would fix her something to eat and she'd hang out for a little while. It was a place where she could feel safe.

She didn't get a lot of details when her mother told her that Gary was her daddy. And this of course made the info even harder to digest. She thought of the decade's worth of visits to the house where she actually belonged all along, and the smiles that came from Sally Helen and my mother and everyone else.

At first it seemed like the greatest betrayal. Why hadn't anyone spoken up? Why hadn't these people claimed her when so much was going on in her childhood? How could such nice folks just abandon one of their own? Especially Gary, who was her godfather at the very least. The truth, however, was not that simple.

"I remember that Granddaddy and Ma-ma [Sally] used to look at me funny. And I used to think that they didn't like me. Yet Sally-Mom always wanted me to go up there and I would be like 'For what?' and she'd be like 'Because they want to see you.' And I didn't understand why. Then I found out when I was about eighteen and it all made sense.

"My mother explained that she wanted to tell me but she never wanted to hurt the feelings of the father and grandfather I already knew because they loved me so much. She knew I was Gary's baby. Everybody was telling her that I looked like Gary, too. But she begged Gary and everybody else not to say anything. Granddaddy [Jesse] was mad at her about that because I was his granddaughter and it wasn't right that I didn't know the truth. But when I realized that God puts everybody through stuff for a reason, maybe that's the way God wanted for me to live."

Jeanette's childhood was a run through a never-ending gauntlet. Her mother had her as a teenager but got it together enough to join the police force, which provided the steady check she needed to keep ends meeting. She took Jeanette and her two little brothers, Stephen and Tristan, to museums and on other cultural outings. Her mom wanted her daughter to see all the world had to offer, and then some. Life, for those first ten years, was pretty sweet.

Then around the time Jeanette was in the fifth grade, her mom was introduced to her good friend Lady Heroin (later followed by Cousin Crack). She got dropped from the force to work full-time as an addict. After that it didn't take much time for mother and family to end up on the streets.

My cousin's wonder years were spent waking up in a different place every few nights. On one occasion she had the pleasure of finding her mother OD'ing on the living room floor. Though her mother didn't die, the scene was enough to alter young Jeanette forever, especially when the incident didn't even slow her mother's addiction. By junior high, Jeanette was often left somewhere with nothing but the keys. No food, no clothes to change into, and two much younger brothers who had fewer answers than she did: it was a much darker version of my other grandfather's life. She was the eldest child having to do it all because no one else could.

"I want to say that it wasn't my mother's fault, that I understand, but the truth is I don't. We lived all over the city, NW, NE, SE, everywhere but SW. But I never was a bad child. I did a lot of things on my own. I was a majorette and played alto sax in the jazz band and the marching band. I went to school, always worked, and still dealt with all the same struggles every other kid does until I was grown."

It brings me a smile to know that she learned to play an instrument, one of her father's all but forgotten dreams. It is believed in the culture of Ifa, the belief system born in West Africa long before Christ, that we are often brought to Earth to succeed where those before us have failed. Jeanette seems to be a shining example of such.

Still, sitting there, I try to count the number of times I've heard this kind of story: a Black child not knowing her father because of a mother's fear, or a father's irresponsibility, or death, or imprisonment, or him walking the streets talking to himself as he still tries to come down from some bad acid trip that started in '74. How do you reverse not knowing your model for the opposite sex? What criteria do you use when searching for the person you want to be with? Do you rely on intuition or base your choices on what's around you: that cute guy on the corner doing hand-to-hand crack sales, the streetball hoop star with dreams of an NBA deal that everybody wants a piece of, the "grimy nigga" who gets away with everything?

The questions become even more complicated when your only parent is a drug addict with nothing but her habit to speak of. What becomes of your definition of home? How do you come to define family? Is the value of a maternal embrace the same when it's followed by the chase for a fix? And the most important question: How do all these things affect your judgment when you've got a baby on the way?

At thirty, Jeanette has three children by multiple fathers and a little brother to take care of. Each of the fathers has come and gone, and she's doing it all on her own. It's the same old story scored by statistics that don't lie. Even among my own generally middle-class group of friends, few know their fathers, and out of those who do, the relationships are distant and often strained. The proof always comes in my dad's visits to wherever I am. I can never let go of the way my friends all surround him, often hanging on his every word, many wishing that they'd had a man like him in their lives.

Yet I in no way want to portray the Black women that keep our community alive as inadequate parents. Nor do I subscribe to any of the trumped-up theories that the blame rests on any one gender, or any one leader, or anything other than the paths and the choices the Creator lays out for each of us. We are all given choices moment to moment, dilemmas that determine not only our own futures, but those of children too young to choose for themselves. Generations of parents have taken their pick and we've ended up with the world of today.

"Motherhood made me really responsible and mature, even though I had already grown up taking care of my brothers. My children mean so much to me. They are the future. All the kids, not just mine. Day to day that's all I worry about, where I'm going and what I can do to be more productive in general and in their lives specifically, especially since I have a three-year-old, Destiny, who has Down syndrome. I still feel like I can change the world, that I can do something that's better than what I'm doing now. And that's all I think about, making the world change for my children.

"I had them young, starting when I was seventeen, and I came from a dysfunctional family. But they were never hungry, never dirty, and never cold."

Now she has an apartment and works whenever she can. She's also set to host a syndicated music video show and plans to spend some of the next few months doing some modeling locally.

"When I was a little girl I always thought it was too expensive for people to have a phone or have some food in their refrigerator. But what I know now is that it is very easy. The way I grew up really made me want to change and to change my children so that they can know more than I did and be more aware of the world."

That, however, is not where her awareness ends. There are far greater struggles beyond the minefield of keeping things afloat.

"I was just talking to a friend of mine about it. Why is the world like this? Why aren't Black people more united as a community? Why are they scared to say they're from Africa? We say we're African American but we're *African*. And that conflict goes into everything else we have to deal with: jobs, schools. And these younger kids don't care, even though they're not going to have it any better. They don't remember that just thirty or forty years ago we were fighting to have the right to an education, or to ride the bus. They don't care about terrorism or the president or all of these laws that are being switched around. They're killing people left and right all over the world and they just don't care. And the killers are getting younger and younger. These young girls out here have

AIDS. So we need to move the younger ones in another direction."

We both have a similarly fatalistic vision of the future, of neo-totalitarian governments telling us when we can and can't go out in the daylight, of G.W. Bush clones ruling the roost for the rest of our lives. We wonder if there will ever be a safe place for our kids to play, or if we'll have to dress them in body armor for the walk to the closest public school. Maybe we've known each other for the longest time beneath the surface. She's the playmate I always dreamed of on many a Sunday evening. And I could have been there for her all of those years when she felt like she had no one.

The cynic in me says that it's too little and too late. But the echoes of my ancestors tell me that it's never too late to bind with your bloodline. There's always time to reforge broken chains. Perhaps the Lone Ranger's death created an opportunity to bring us closer. He was the one who petitioned the most for her rejoining our clan. Now it's up to us, those who remain, to keep her here. Perhaps she and I can each still be the cousin the other longed for.

The greatest difference between us is that I know the Langleys. Jeanette's knowledge is rather scattered. At least I had those moments with my grandfather up in the room and out on the porch. At least I had his stubbly embrace whenever I wanted it.

"He kept calling me all the time wanting me to come over in those last years," she says. "I kept saying I was going to go over there. I felt really bad because he'd always call. He used to say it was real important for me to know my people. But I was like 'They don't know me and I don't know them.' "

And that has never stopped getting in the way. She's trying a little harder now, but getting acquainted with family you haven't known for thirty years isn't the easiest task. I tell her that I'm there for her. I just hope she truly hears me.

It's hard for us to convey our feelings when the tape stops. The door between us has creaked open a little wider. We stand and hug, holding each other for as long as courtesy will allow before I watch her leave, going off into the night the way she came. All dreams can come true. But only in their own time.

2

I am seated in the basement of a church somewhere in Stamford, Connecticut. The audience is mostly female, Black women in their forties and fifties who have come out to support two young men, positive brothers who have chosen to be writers, writers who wanted a chance to be read beyond their own circles of influence.

I feel out of place as I observe the other positive young brother on the bill execute his plan of attack for generating better book sales. His game plan is to woo the women before him with a clichéd hard luck story about everything it took for him to get his book into print, about how racist the publishing racket is and how much of the material they wanted him to change. I find his presentation to be nauseatingly pretentious and tacky. Yet the crowd is loving it. After all there isn't a sista in the world who doesn't want to see a brother win, no matter what story he might spin.

I, however, am from a different school of thought. I believe that writers should let their words speak for themselves. Plus I'm a little too shy to go the sermon route. So as I wait for my turn, as I wait for my chance to offer up what I've created to an audience of complete strangers in hopes that they just might buy a few of the volumes I've got stashed in my bag, I have no clue as to how it's going to turn out.

My colleague in letters takes a seat to roaring applause, the kind of claps mothers give sons after they've done something good. I'm up next. But before I grab the mic a young woman about my age appears at the podium. She's a little thing just over five feet and cute as a button. Were I single there might be plotting for her digits. But I'm not. There's also a diamond on the proper finger. And as I learn from her brief introduction, she just happens to be my second cousin.

I don't particularly know what to think of this. It's even more awkward when she points out various faces in the crowd. They are family and friends of family and people who those friends of family may have mentioned me to. Yet, as usual, I see them all as strangers, an ocean of aliens who speak a language I'm far from familiar with. My boyhood shyness takes hold and I wish I could just escape, go off to some other room filled with complete strangers, someplace where I'm just Kenji the writer and not Sally Helen's daughter's only son.

Still, I give them a very big smile, not just because I don't want to offend them, but also because it's what I wish came naturally. I should know these people. I should be happy to see them. Suddenly I understand Jeanette's dilemma wholeheartedly. Suddenly I see how much history slips through our fingers. We don't make the connections. We don't take the time, and before we know it the time will be up.

My newfound second cousin is genuinely nervous as she says a few words, reading what's been written in the program about me, a relation she doesn't know. She retreats as I approach. And then we hug, both visibly feeling a little awkward. She goes to her seat and I go to the lectern and read. Afterward we do exchange phone numbers and promise to fill in all the gaps. It is April of 2003. It is more than a year before I make the call and arrange to visit her at her home in Connecticut.

Latanya Langley was born on July 26, 1975, barely four months before I came into the world. She is the daughter of Betty and Curtis Langley (Curtis being the Langley brother I missed on my last trip to Norwalk). She is the middle child, ten years younger than her elder brother and ten older than her younger male sibling. She knew what she wanted almost from the day she emerged from the womb: to be an attorney, which she is at a prestigious national law firm she'd rather not name. But for her this is only a starting point.

This only daughter was raised in Norwalk as if she had everything, as if her parents (neither of whom had more than a high school diploma) had all the money in the world. She attended the best private schools in the area: St. Joseph's for grade school and junior high, and then on to St. Luke's for high school. Next came four undergrad years at Trinity College, one year at the London School of Economics, and three more at UConn Law.

In DuBoisian theory, Latanya would be considered a part of the "talented tenth," the supposed highest echelon of African American society. The "tenth" are born and reared to educate and uplift the masses of African Americans. They are the ones who will strike the greatest blows against racial, social, and economic oppression.

She sits before me in her living room knowing this, knowing that she is the embodiment of strength and determination, the sum of God and her parents' near-perfect planning. It's not so much in her words as it is in her demeanor. She knows that she has worked hard, that she chose to study on the nights everyone else went out to the party. She knows that her every word and action might be scrutinized by friend and foe alike. She knows that there is never rest for the truly weary. Yet none of these things makes her any less happy to be where she is.

Her house was so Christian growing up that church and school a0re almost all she can remember. Her formative years were packed solid with hard wood pews and brass collection plates, prayer meetings and Bible studies. She was that little girl sandwiched between her parents, both of whom always testified to the goodness of the Lord. Her father's child, she easily filled juvenile versions of his shoes. Father held his Greenville values dear; as his daughter, Latanya followed suit.

When she wasn't in church, she was playing volleyball, basketball, and softball or learning the piano and every kind of dance. Activity and exercise took the place of interaction with her peers. She was not allowed to play with boys. She didn't even get to talk to friends on the phone or sleep over at girl-friends' houses.

See, Curtis knew the world in which his child was being reared. The smallest thing could be just enough to knock his little girl off the righteous path. He was *not* going to let that happen. There was no way.

"If a guy gave me a gift, like if a boy handed me a lollipop, I'd have to give it back," she remembers. "He taught me never to take anything from a boy because they always had ulterior motives. He always taught me to be with someone who has equal to or more than what I had, whether that was financially or spiritually. He always taught me to be independent and not need a man for anything. If I wanted something, I had to work for it because he wouldn't give it to me or let anyone else give it to me. I had to work for the five dollars it cost me to buy my first bike at a garage sale."

Her mother, Betty, is Curtis's perfect counterpart. Quiet and humble, she keeps the house together, trimming all the ends before they even get close to coming loose. Mother and daughter prayed together at night, side by side on their knees next to the little girl's mattress. The mother loves her daughter more than anything and is more than proud of all she's accomplished in her first thirty years. Betty is always in the audience, always clapping and cheering and thanking the Lord for all the blessings he's rained down upon her daughter.

From the outside looking in, Latanya's life is the stuff of dreams. She rises every morning to the realization of her own childhood fantasies. As early as age five she'd use her dolls to play "court" on her bedroom floor. At six her grandmother's strongest prayers were for her to grow up to be the best attorney the world ever saw.

Yet there's a downside to it all, one stealthed by the résumé and material possessions. Unlike the majority of us, she can shop on Fifth Avenue every once in a while. Maybe she's closer than us to the luxury automobiles it's customary for us to drool over. But the thing that she can't stop thinking about is how alone she is up there. It often seems as if her success has placed two worlds and the moon on her shoulders.

"I was always the only Black person from elementary to middle school to high school all the way up to undergrad and law school," she says. "Practicing law, I've always been one of a handful. And although I was considered a part of the chosen few, it was lonely because I didn't have anyone in the family who had gone before me and experienced those things. My father hadn't already been a lawyer and my grandfather didn't have a college degree. My colleagues had had that. So with everything I did, I was always the one breaking ground and making all the mistakes so that whoever came behind me would have someone. I never had anyone before me who experienced racism in higher education or racism within the executive class. I was ignorant of many things that were common to the average person in the world I was trying to become a part of."

At a time when much of what we're calling hip-hop informs us that the hood is all that matters, that how you represent your town or your street or the set of projects where you were reared is a gauge for your Blackness, a person can feel a sense of isolation when she doesn't have baby-daddy problems or "thug love" with a brother who can't find a job because of his criminal record. If you're upwardly mobile without the use of Hollywood, the NBA, or the music industry, then you're perceived as a sell-out or a "bourgie" or someone who just wants to be white.

Latanya's plight is one often ignored by the community at large, particularly beyond her own circles. It gets even tougher when relationships come into the mix. All you have to do is check the statistics and you'll learn that more than half of Black women under forty will not get married in the course of their lifetime. And even if you ignore the stats, every Black woman's magazine drives the point home for you every other issue.

Even here Latanya was blessed, or at least she seemed to be at first. A nice enterprising man met her gaze when she was the tender age of twenty-four. She and this man married in September of 2001 and filed for a divorce in June of 2004.

"I fell in love with a guy who had all the credentials that I required of a man. He had higher degrees. He was very good-looking. And I thought he was spiritual, which made him a very good trophy for me. As long as he had those things, I thought we had a good marriage. But because I was so young and naive, I forgot to look at his soul and really watch his spirit to see if he was connected to God."

Somewhere in those three years she discovered that he had a "substance abuse issue" that ran the risk of putting all of his credentials in jeopardy. Then she remembered what substance abuse had done to her family. Her grandfather, Willie Langley, the Lone Ranger's older brother, was an alcoholic, a once kind man who had wreaked havoc on her grandmother, Hattie. Though those times had come long before her, their effects reverberated through the lives and marriages of all three of her aunts, all of whom are now divorced. Thinking about all of this and keeping her father's warnings about men in mind, she decided that she couldn't deal.

"I didn't love him enough to go down that path with him," she says of her husband. "He was in denial. He wouldn't get help. He'd gotten this far with his habit, so there was no real reason for him to change. So I told him if he didn't get help I was going to divorce him. And he didn't. So I divorced him."

She's quite relieved now, although she misses the good times. A man who is not willing to take care of his problems is more of a liability than an asset. Plus, the more she thinks about it, the whole thing was a business relationship. She thought there was love in the beginning, but now that the fog of circumstance has cleared, she's not so sure.

"I thought I was in love when I was dating him. But I thought that with the guy before him too. I'd dropped him as well because he was supposed to be going to law school but decided to become a teacher. I didn't do it because of his choice. I did it because of the reasons for the choice. He chose teaching because he didn't want to put forth the effort to become the lawyer he wanted to be."

Perhaps she went into womanhood searching for someone like her father, a man who worked himself to the bone for her, and is still working. Perhaps her mistakes with men were in choosing the suit of shining armor without lifting the helmet to see what was inside. If so, she wouldn't be the first to do so.

In the race to do better, to overcome the socioeconomic odds facing Black families, so many sistas come into adulthood searching for Supermen who can help them afford the trappings that accompany success, charismatic specimens who can fill the void of fathers who fell out of reach before they were born.

So they scour the happy hours and churches and cultural events, the corporate luncheons and faculty receptions, in search of what looks like the answer. They so rarely know that wolves have learned to dress in great-guy clothing—that is, until they finally peel out of their suits. After that revelation it doesn't take long for these women to head back to the dating pool.

I envy my grandfather in this regard. In his time there were few expectations in comparison. A good man had a good job, a strong back, and faith in the Lord. A good woman knew how to cook good meals, tend to the kids, and support her husband in every way that she could. Having "issues" meant you were sick, disabled, or out of your mind. Everything didn't have a category. Navigating relationships didn't require checklists, how-to books, or appointments with psychotherapists.

That's not to say that marriages were better for that generation. Sally Helen and Jesse and Hattie and Willie and even

Melvin and Angela are proof that the past is in no way superior to the present. There are still so many issues for us beneath the surface, fragments lodged within the grimy crevices of our experience. We were broken by those who controlled us, and coming together in any way, not to mention romantically, doesn't just happen with a fifth of Hennessey and R. Kelly on the stereo.

I have literally watched women I love lose their minds. I have visited women with the perfect balance of beauty, wit, and intelligence in hospital psych wards. I have built coalitions to stave off eating disorders and suicide attempts by grown up little girls whose fathers disowned them long ago. And as I've said before, so many of my male peers are no better off as they try to become men without proper models, aspiring like fictional characters because living a fantasy has to be better than living an empty vacuum.

Sanity and what is normal have become relative only to the nightly news, prime-time TV, and witty banter at the water cooler. It makes me think of the sermons of so many of the preachers I heard during my childhood. They always spoke of the last days coming, of man's arrogance being his undoing. It seems as if almost everything we've learned comes with vicious side effects, from the food we manufacture to the images we broadcast across the planet via media suspected to be giving us all cancer. Love is no longer an emotion but a painful task we must endure, and making a family has become a high-wire act without a net down below.

"I see a lot of Black women being in very passionate relationships, either passionately in love or passionately in pain. Thus, I don't see a lot of relationships lasting a long time. I think that's because most of the women are more willing to walk away than they would have been in the past. And a lot of Black men are willing to take risks on their relationships with the hope of not getting caught. Black women are getting wiser. Before they'd stay because of the kids, or because they couldn't afford to leave. Before they were putting up with the crap. But they're not staying anymore, because they don't feel like they have to. You don't get shunned anymore for leaving."

Latanya, however, knows that she'll get it right the next time. Because now she knows that love is more than credentials, that her mate's soul will hold the truths of all that he is. Until she meets the right guy, she and her nearly perfect profile of beauty, brains, and financial stability have to keep it moving, especially when there's so much work to do.

"I'm trying to get my family to see beyond where they came from and see where they are," she remarks. "A lot of them are stuck in where they were raised and how they were raised. They don't want to advance even when there's so many talented and business-minded folks around them.

"The biggest challenge for our community is not repeating in this generation the same mistakes our ancestors made. We still have a slave mentality in many ways. It's just a different kind of slave mentality. For example, a lot of us are now in college but we still feel like we're inferior. We go to job interviews with the attitude that we're not as qualified as the next man purely because of the color of our skin, or at least we allow ourselves to be treated that way. We also get caught up in working for other people because that's all we know. There aren't enough of us willing to start our own thing, to build our own empires. So we're still working for The Man. We're afraid to use our creativity because we're in fear of being rejected. A lot of us stop when we get our first job out of high school and don't go to college, or we stop at college. The drugs and the music were different in past generations but it feels like we're re-creating the same issues over and over again."

Unlike so many, Latanya can proudly say that she's part of the solution rather than part of the problem. At thirty she has more than her father has in his near sixty years. In a way she's actually living his dream by achieving everything he wanted for her and more. She's also allowing him to live dreams of his own by writing him checks whenever they're needed, most recently contributing to the tuition for her younger brother and assisting him in his run at a college degree in business.

Her words generate responses of my own. Here I am ninety minutes above the Rotten Apple, leaning back against the couch of another stranger I should know far better than I do. We rattle off lists of family that the other only vaguely recognizes. We speak on college, adulthood, and women and men. Many of our opinions have a nice bit of symmetry, others the clashing bells of disagreement.

Unlike Jeanette, Latanya has always been within reach. It would only have taken the Lone Ranger asking me to tag along on one of his frequent trips to Norwalk. She remembers him coming, particularly how much he and Willie looked alike. For her, it's hard to believe that that guy was my grandfather, as if the two of us wouldn't belong together if placed in the same frame.

Though I am not an attorney or in possession of a master's (despite my dear mother's wishes), I too am a center of pride for those who carry the Langley name. I too have stood alone as an achiever in foreign worlds. Once again I find myself admitting that I could have used the company.

It isn't as if our not being introduced was anything intentional. Jesse and Sally Helen's family almost never came together at the same time. Connecticut might as well have been

California in the mind of any born and bred Washingtonian, particularly the ones in my bunch.

"It must have been really hard for you," she says about my grandfather dying before we could do a book together.

I try to be a tough guy. I try to pretend that it still doesn't hurt a little, that my understanding that he is looking down on me every moment of the day shields me from any feeling of loss. Still, she sees right through it, so I tell her how much it pains me, that because of his death, this excursion had to become something very different, something very unexpected. Instead of getting all the answers in a nice and orderly fashion, I'm combing corners and closets for residue, tracking down little bits of flotsam and jetsam in hopes of making a collage instead of compiling the perfect portrait of him that might have been, had he continued living. Still, it is what it is. Life has to go on.

"Ten years from now I want to be married with three children," she proclaims, changing the subject. "But I lost focus when I got married and forgot to take care of me. Now I want to be a judge and a professor. I should have been a congresswoman or a mayor or something like that already. We should always be aiming for upward mobility. . . . You've got to get involved in politics. I think every Black man should go to law school, even if he doesn't practice law. Go out on the golf course just because you couldn't do it before. You have to speak out. You have to hope."

The Lone Ranger just wanted a house, a car, and the money to make it all work for the kids. That was a lot for a Black man with no education or any real plan. Two generations later we want the world. And some of us have actually garnered a little slice, though the majority still struggle for what he wanted. The majority of us are still trying to get our forty acres and a mule, just a fistful of crumbs from America's pie.

Many of us who have achieved can see only the road ahead, the other things we want, the other issues we want to tackle, the next seats up the ladder we want to fill. We often forget that we left so much chaos behind us, that there are so many who can use our expertise to get things back on track, who need to see that there are other alternatives besides the handful of options they've been told they have to choose from.

On the A train back to Brooklyn, I eavesdrop on conversations. A girl my age is plotting to get her supervisor fired. A brother in his thirties tells his wife how much he didn't like the Sunday brunch from which they're returning. A white police trainee complains to his Latin counterpart about the weight of his Beretta firearm and how he wants to get a Glock as soon as he can afford it.

The air brings these words to me as a reminder of how large life's playing field can be. We as people are separated by geography, class, race, and outlook. So many times I'll listen to voices in the crowd and feel like Armageddon will hit my doorstep next Tuesday. Then I wonder if I'm the only one who knows this, the only one who sees the destructive patterns that are taking our world apart.

On this train my thoughts are not so much of the end of the world but of the way we all live too much of life staring at our own navels. Then I think of Latanya and me, both of us the products of our parents, both of us doing our thing to get beyond where our parents were. She's made it and I'm still trying. But so many aren't.

So many of us are just trapped in the rhythm of our day-to-day, never looking up, never asking why but instead waiting for that manna to fall from heaven again instead of baking it ourselves. For so many, praying for anything more than health and survival is asking for too much. Aiming to surpass instead of merely meeting the status quo is seen as being unsatisfied, unless it's an endless quest for the material items flaunted before us on the E channel or in the latest music video.

There are folks who climb out of bed each day with a plan. Others know what they don't want but can't for the life of them figure out what they do. There are some who hit the Snooze button until it comes off. But there are a selected few who rise, with a plan, who see the day-to-day as a means to a larger end, who use the past to bring about change in the ever-approaching future. Which of these people should we be? And how do we evolve without losing our minds in the process?

3

Hospitals reek of everything and nothing: the countless drugs and fluids, the chemicals and agents used to save lives mixed with the stillness of the dead, of those unfortunate temples found to be beyond rescue. One cannot forget the fake smiles from nurses and orderlies who've been on their feet for twelve hours straight, nor the laughs and grunts of patients who'd rather be somewhere else.

It's almost five on a rainy Thursday in downtown DC. Georgetown is one way and the White House the other.

Across the street, in an older ward of this same facility, lies the place where I came into the world, its outer structure now named after a recently departed former president I've always despised. But that's all in the past. I'm here for the future.

Jesse James Langley III (aka Lil' Jay), the Lone Ranger's namesake, comes alive as I enter Room 531. His left leg is elevated and wrapped in a brace. This is his third visit to this facility since he injured himself while running hurdles in a track meet at the beginning of summer. Five months later, he's still in the throes of recovery, and may continue to be for months or even years to come.

The hardest part for him is not being able to move, his inability to travel from any one room to the next at his usual lightning speed. Movement is what he's always taken pride in, because as an athlete, speed and momentum have been of the utmost importance to him.

He could outshoot me in free throws on a Playskool hoop before he was three. By the time I was twenty-five and he was thirteen, I couldn't beat him in a ten-second race with a two-minute start. Now that he's eighteen I wouldn't even try. The spitting image of his father, he is still lean and muscular even after months of not training. This is the hardest thing he's ever had to face, that his dreams of athletic glory may never come to fruition, that the scholarship that allowed him to attend St. Albans, one of the most respected and revered private schools in the nation, may mark his end rather than his beginning. That, however, is a sidebar to why I'm here. He and the Lone Ranger are the real story.

While I learned what I knew of our grandfather from two Sunday visits per month, Lil' Jay got to know him every day in the time they lived together when he was little. Truth be told, it is Sally Helen whom he calls "Ma," and her lap in which he still

rests even though he is now
twice the woman's size. He
was the one to find the body,
the poor soul who discovered
that the Langleys' head of
household had passed on.

His grandfather had been
in the tub longer than usual,
so Jay went up to check on
him. He opened the bath-
room door to find Jesse's head
beneath the soapy water. He
immediately called for help
and Gary quickly scaled the

*Jay at two and me at fourteen on a
summer visit to Powhatan, Virginia.*

stairs to pull him out. By the time paramedics arrived, Jesse Sr.
was already gone, though they could find no exact cause of
death, even after two separate autopsies.

"I didn't know how to deal with finding him like that," Jay
mumbles, reliving the moment. "I look at a lot of TV so I get
a lot of my emotions from a lot of the stuff I see on TV. And
on TV everybody cries when someone dies, so I think I sub-
consciously made myself start crying."

He told himself that it was his fault, that he should have
come up to check on his grandfather sooner, that maybe if he
had, maybe Jesse Sr. would still be here. He told himself that
because there was nothing else he could possibly say. The first
man he ever knew was gone, and there was nothing anyone
on this earth could do about it.

Like too many young Black boys, he barely knew his father growing up. After he was no longer with Jay's mother, Junie would come by to visit his son on Childress Street, staying
only an hour or two, that time shared between the child and

everyone else. It wasn't that Junie meant to be neglectful. He was only drawing on what he knew. His father hadn't been there day to day. He was out working or upstairs sleeping. Still, a young boy in the '90s knew nothing about that history. Jay became frustrated without even knowing it.

His grandfather, however, was always there. Even if he didn't say much he was seated on the couch or out on the porch or in fussing with Sally Helen. There were times when he spoke to Jay. He loved to tell the story of John Hunley, a distant cousin of Sally Helen's mother, Lucy, and how he stepped off a train in Richmond coming from Long Island looking to make a name for himself. Hunley, though Jesse had never met him, was someone he identified with. They had both left home in search of something new. They both hungered for a better life, went after it and got it.

Jesse Sr. told his grandson about how much he loved baseball and how men weren't supposed to have long hair and how women weren't supposed to be in the pulpit and a million other things that didn't make much sense to a little boy, words spoken in a language he was too young to understand.

During Jay's first two years at St. Albans Jesse would pick him up and take him home for the weekend. The man was always on time and always parked in the same exact place. Jay remembers, toward the end of his years at Ruth K. Webb, when Jesse pulled up with a flat tire the two of them had to patch in the rain. Then, once the rain stopped and they were on their way home, Jesse strangely decided to stop and pick up a lady fare that took them almost an hour away from the house. Then he took them to a tire place to get a new tire to replace the one they'd patched. For a ten-year-old that ride seemed like it would never end.

"I got home from school three hours after I was supposed to," Jay remembers, "but all I could do was laugh."

Still Jay admits that there could have been plenty of other opportunities for him to learn more about the man. But like our uncle Tony before him, Jay was always more concerned with protecting Sally Helen, the woman he loves more than anything. His grandfather was always yelling at her and he used to get drunk a lot. The boy seemed to spend half his time calming her down, trying to create a distraction away from the man she'd married when she was barely out of high school, so that the conflict would end.

He didn't know what to think about it. Sally Helen and Jesse were the only couple he ever got to watch through his early years. Though what was going on didn't seem right to him, it was all he knew, thus there wasn't much for him to think about. It was what it was, all the way until the end.

"I knew him as a grandson but not in the way his friends knew him. And now that he's gone I miss him being here. I didn't know he meant so much to the people in this house and in keeping the family together."

Since his grandfather's death, Jay has seen how broken the family has become, how everyone is still struggling to find their place in his absence, how it just doesn't feel the same inside of his grandma's house. There's an emptiness there now. When you sit or stand or climb the stairs to use the house's only bathroom, you're waiting to see Granddad, to smell the cigarettes and Polo cologne, to hear him call the name of whichever child or grandchild he needs to speak to from his abode at the rear. Yet the call doesn't come. Still, you look and listen and wait for it upon each and every visit.

"I'm learning that I'm kinda like him," Jay says with the straightest of faces. "I'm kinda old-fashioned."

Jay and I in 2004 at poet Millery Polyne's Jazz Night in Harlem.

A devout member of Spirit of Christ Baptist Church, Jay has very few friends and prefers spending time around his family to being out at some high school house party. He saves every dollar he gets and enjoys the peace and quiet of his own thoughts. Perhaps he is the man come again. Perhaps the Lone Ranger has found the means to view his flock from the other side. But when it comes to the ladies, Jay is his daddy's child. His voice sinks to Barry White depths each of the three times his cell phone rings.

Jay now lives with his mother, Karen, in the Carriage Hill Apartments just across the DC border in Hillcrest Heights, Maryland. Childress Street is no longer his home, though it's still in his heart. With a bedroom of basketball and football posters and a closet of athletic gear, sports has been his life. He doesn't have to get over his shyness on a field or ball court. The moves just come to him, as does his sense of humor. He answers Sally Helen's phone in fake deep and shrill voices. Whenever I tell him I'm working on something, his eyes come alive and he struts through the house like a teenaged P. Diddy, telling everyone that my "next joint is going platinum!" For him there's a joke in everything, even if his kidding occasionally manages to try his older cousin's patience.

But now, stretched across a mechanical bed for the third time in as many months, he's being forced to accept the fact that he may have to make his life's mark in another arena. Knee injuries can take years to heal. And as a high school senior, *years* could wipe out his eligibility for athletic scholarships to college.

"I just want to be successful at anything I do," Jay tells me. "Whenever I'm at school or doing homework, I'm thinking to myself that I have to support my family and make sure that my kids are taken care of after I die. That's what means the most to me and that's what I think success is."

He also knows that so many of his peers are not succeeding. So many kids are getting caught up. Carriage Hill is not a place where young people are dying every day, but so many of them are drinking and using drugs. He knows of one boy two years older than him who started smoking cigarettes a year ago. Now he's a full-blown crackhead.

Many of the youth are without guidance. Many are influenced by the same songs they hear twelve times an hour encouraging them to smoke weed, drink champagne, have uncommitted sex, kill people, rob people, and fly all around the world with the money this makes them. Sure, plenty of youth and adults are working hard, studying and doing what they're supposed to do, but there aren't enough of them.

"I can talk some more." He giggles as the interview comes to a close. I smile with him though he can tell that I'm being serious, trapped in my journalist/writer/let's-get-this-right mode. Then, just as he gets a straight face, he explodes into laughter. When I ask him why, all he can offer is a shrug of the shoulders.

"I laugh at everything because that's the best way to get through things," he responds. Thus begins the eighteen-year-old outline for happiness.

"See, to me, if you want to be happy, you're going to be happy. If you don't, you're not."

He's been under observation for four days, trapped between four walls with no books and bad hospital TV. The post-surgery infection in his knee has been neutralized and it's time to go home. He gets himself into the wheelchair as I carry his crutches, his mother right behind us. My mother is waiting at the front of the building to take the two of them home. I am headed back to Brooklyn, to bring all this to a close in the only way I know how.

On the way down I tell him not to worry about his leg, that he'll be back training again in no time. I tell him that he's going to get into Morehouse and that I'll do everything I can for him. He smiles as his mother and I load him into the rear of my mother's Geo Metro. Then he pats me on the shoulder and says, "I know."

I stand there in the nastiness of the autumn mist and watch the car disappear into Wednesday's rush hour. I have been to DC more times this year than the last five combined. I've logged hours of tape and ridden buses and trains until my ass felt raw. Now I have to go home and put it all together. I bang on keyboards all the way to Penn Station, thinking on my mother and uncles, my father, Jeanette, and Sally Helen, and of my unborn child, unnamed and with a future yet to be written. They all make up a sphere of possibilities, a fiery globe of a vision I must now make real.

4

It's after 4 a.m. on November 3, 2004, and I am somewhere deep in Flatbush, Brooklyn. The rum, smoke, fatigue, and my state of shock make the further details a blur. The only clarity is found in the music in my head, the imperial march from the *Star Wars* trilogy. Bush has been elected to another term. The Empire has truly struck back.

My good friend Allen puts a fire to the spliff between his fingers. His girlfriend buries herself in his lap, vowing that they're now moving to Vancouver. This is the moment that defines my belief in there being two Americas, one *theirs* and one *ours*. And despite the best efforts of every sensible entertainer under the sun, or every word penned by every writer, and every picture shot by every photographer, and every line rhymed by every MC within these fifty states, there are more of *them*. This is a democracy. Therefore they, the majority, get what they want.

We came close, but we didn't make it, even when there were enough of us to take them down. This kind of thing makes me refill my glass in disgust.

The Lone Ranger was not born with the right to vote. He didn't even earn it when he turned eighteen. He was forty-six years old when the Voting Rights Act of '65 was passed, which meant he lived more than half his life disenfranchised, as did most of those he knew.

He entered buildings via separate entrances, or in some cases, never at all. When he drove, he took Route 1 to stay out of harm's way, and he always worked two jobs to bring in what a white man could earn with one. He did all of this with no five-year plan or résumé, no degrees from accredited institutions, no pension, and not even the guarantee of a raise after a given passing of time.

He cleared the roads as he traveled them. There was no family business for him to inherit. There was no summer job waiting for him at sixteen because his parents had friends who could do them favors. He never got to jump the line because someone had a reason to look the other way.

Jesse James Langley, Sr., was one of the last of an era that is beyond its twilight, of a time and place in which the effort you made mattered more than your credentials or pedigree. He was a boy from a hick town who threw his chips on the table and pushed them all in because he wouldn't settle for anything less.

He begat Angela and Junie and Gary, who in turn begat myself, Lil' Jay, and Jeanette. He instilled the values in his own that kept food on our tables, and the idea that doing nothing was perhaps the greatest sin of all. We, his grandchildren, along with Latanya, his great-niece, stand before the walls of what we think is right, preparing to defend it against an onslaught of everything that is not.

I rise from my homeboy's couch, give him a half-hug good-bye and stumble out into the night, praying for a morning that does not come, a morning when the tally of blue states outnumbers the red.

The shuttle train to Franklin Avenue is all brothers at three in the morning, men in their forties and fifties. The stubble on their faces has grayed, their clothing is wrinkled and torn, their eyes are glazed over as if there's no difference between yesterday and tomorrow. Where are they going and where did they come from? Where were they when their sons and daughters needed them?

The Lone Ranger lived life on a schedule. Arrivals and departures were consistent, if not predictable. There was work, then home, then sleep, maybe room for a few words to the kids somewhere along the way, or *Bonanza*, if he was lucky. His three boys learned his schedule. They felt that rhythm. They knew what it was that they were supposed to do, just by his being there.

Still, rhythm and direction do not foster warmth. They don't give a child a sense of belonging. They don't answer all the questions a young soul needs to mature. Providing the elements for survival is only one part of fatherhood. Nurturing the mind and the spirit is a far more complicated other necessity. I'm sure he did the best he could, but I know in my heart that it was not enough.

Like James Marvin said up in Norwalk, Jesse's children haven't stuck together. They do not embrace. They do not check in with one another the way the Norwalk Langley boys do. Their interactions, though often filled with humor and good times, can be cold and distant, except when it comes to Sally Helen. She gets all the kisses and laughs and hugs she can stand. She is their heart, but in their minds they are their father's children.

I could be wrong about all these things. My observations could be over the top and untrue. But I'd like to think I have my mother's heart, which came to her from Sally Helen. And that heart says I'm dead-on.

Every child leaves the nest with scars, and Sally Helen and Jesse undoubtedly left their young with a few scrapes, mostly in the form of a lack of answers, a deficient sense of what it means to be a man or woman in the outer world. They all compensated in their own ways. Junie became fixated on himself. My mother became fixated on others. Gary fell in love with the needle, and Tony dedicated himself to keeping his loved ones happy.

I wish God had given my grandfather a few more months, long enough for me to corroborate as much of this as I could. But maybe if he had remained alive these questions would not have been so pertinent, more of a need than a literary and anthropological desire. Or maybe the answers he would've given would've been baffling. The Lone Ranger was a man from a time and place that is practically extinct, an era based on the values of the Good Book before they were building churches the size of football stadiums, before family values became a political platform, before everything had a label, analysis, and conclusion.

His people walked more than they drove. They never ate out. They washed clothes on a board in a tin tub and hung them out to dry. They trusted in the advice of the elders instead of the columns in celebrity magazines. And they worked until they couldn't work anymore, laying the foundation for children who would fight for the chance for more, for the right to be treated equally, for living, loving, and owning property the way their ancestors had so long before. Yet, as it turned out, those children were not fully prepared for the impact of the change they would bring about.

Mel Jasper was right about his generation. Coming out of families like the Lone Ranger's, living under marriages just as utilitarian, they wanted a different life for themselves. They wanted true love and their rights and the chance to remake the world over just because they wished it so. Their youth was their weakness; their ambition, their downfall. In the end they got everything they wanted and didn't know what to do with it.

The sistas could do it on their own. The brothas didn't have to get tied down by all the bullshit. For the wins, they would party through a whole decade. The losses would show themselves via our lives for the next thirty years. Teenaged pregnancy skyrocketed, along with drug use, abuse, and the tens of thousands of murders that came out of the crack game.

The best of their leadership did everything to apply brakes to the runaway train. But it was too big and it was moving far too fast. Following their often misguided examples, we made Max Julian and Ron O'Neal our heroes, and reached even higher levels of misogyny by sporting women in collars and leashes at the MTV awards. We idolized Frank White in *King of New York*, and Nino Brown, Henry Hill, and the Corleones because they got away with it and most of us never did.

We chased after our manhood in all the corners and crevices where the tiniest trace of it might remain. We were going to smush it altogether into one complete thing. What we got was a mess, a slimy gelatinous dung heap that we continue to try to work from.

"You wanna go out, daddy?" the woman in front of the bodega asks me. Her thighs are stuffed into pants that can barely hold them. Her breasts hang loose beneath a cheap T-shirt. Her makeup is smeared to cover the acne on her face. It is only in this first time being solicited that I see that this is someone's daughter.

It's a shame she thinks her vagina is the only thing she has worth selling. This could be Latanya's sister. She could live in

Lil' Jay's building or sit in a cubicle across from Jeanette. Here she is out in the street, living the life of a junkie. And here I am, addicted to words. Our lives aren't the same but we've lived through the same box of time, passengers on opposite ends of the same damn boat. I tipsily decline and continue down the block toward my home.

The Lone Ranger didn't care about what the white folks had, or the brand name of the clothes he wore on his back, or if someone on the block happened to cruise by in a brand-new car when his was only used. He was always concerned with what was under the hood, the machinery of things. As long as it ran smoothly he was a happy man.

We, in my generation, on the other hand, want it all now. Seven-figure salaries by twenty-five. If the Neptunes got rich then so should we. If Shaq's got that custom-made Benz with the Superman emblem steering wheel, then so should we. MTV Cribs has become the home window-shopping channel. There are always more things we're wanting, to prove we've made it. More things to prove that we're not caught in the same trap as half the people we know. In the street we'll go in on a heist, a PS2 or a sack of weed, but we won't pool resources to stop the white folks from buying out our neighborhoods.

We won't clean up the trash on the corners we supposedly care about, or even try to say something to the kids buying their meals from bulletproof windows after midnight. But we'll be the first to say how bad the neighborhood is, or to lash out at someone else who tried to make our "around the way" better.

It's as if our parents' legacy came through garbled. We have enough of the history to know it's important, but not enough to understand how special we are. We have so much work to

do if we don't want clowns like our incumbent president ruling the roost forever and peeling away our rights like dried
glue from grade-school fingers.

I'm thinking of hopping a plane to somewhere else. Hey,
Baldwin and Wright did it. So did McKay, Himes, and
Josephine Baker. Hell, Randall Robinson even wrote a book
about it.

As a matter of fact that might be the best plan. Fly out in
the morning and let someone else sort it out. Seems like a
grand idea as my cheek touches goose down pillow. But
something keeps me awake.

Just weeks before I had been to visit my father. The issue
of the state of things came to the forefront, and I'd told him
that I was done, that our community was finished, that these
people I called my peers, who spent their time supporting
flicks like *Soul Plane*, *Diary of a Mad Black Woman*, and the
Wayans Brothers catalog, couldn't care less about changing
things. They were happy with how it all was. They were cool
with remaining ignorant and powerless forever.

Upon hearing my words, Pop just kind of grinned at me.
He had been where I was. He had felt how I felt. But those
feelings passed.

He reminded me that the '60s movement did not begin as
a mass movement. Those who joined in the beginning were
often ignored by their peers and ridiculed for their views and
(later) those stupid-looking Afros. Those names who made the
greatest sacrifices for change were often unsung, and it takes
time for any kind of revolution to get going, especially here
in America.

"This is the center of the world for the diaspora," he
growled. "Every other Black person in the world looks here
to see what we're going to do." It is evidenced through the re-

verberating effect our fight against racial inequality has had across the world, in Zimbabwe and South Africa, in London and Paris, in Cuba and Brazil. Hip-hop is everywhere. The moves we make stretch around the world and back again.

If I believe him, then in truth there is nowhere else to go. The struggle will find me wherever I hide and anger me as much anywhere as it has here. Besides, Buster Jasper did not flee the war in Korea or his struggles for equal treatment from his employers at the Hecht Company.

The Lone Ranger chose to make a name for himself on the streets of Washington, DC. He stood in line for a whole day to get a job driving a milk truck so that he could deliver a better future for those coming behind him.

I carry the blood of women and men who were always ready for war, always prepared to swing until they could swing no more. Thus I will be no different. We will be no different. I drift off to sleep knowing that it's not over, that in actuality it has only just begun.

It's not too late to return to a true definition of community as it was. We remember all the elements that went into making it work. The village raises the child. People keep an eye on things. A neighbor rats you out if he sees you playing with matches, and has the right to cuff you to a chair if you're holding drugs or a pistol.

The blueprint for a better tomorrow has been with us the whole time. We no longer have to wait for someone to rise and lead us. We no longer need charismatic men in suits to tell us how to change things. In every hood, those who want things to be different must find others of like mind. Then those groups must pool their resources to fund the most appropriate actions for change.

This is not to say that five people can change African

America. But I do mean to say that those five folks can get another five going somewhere else, who will in turn do the same, and eventually, whether it is years, decades, or centuries from now, we'll all be on the same page.

This is an era where "right now" passes with every second on the dial. The babies of the babies who had kids in the late '80s are now growing to adulthood. If we don't get our act together, how much worse will it get and how quickly?

This isn't just about voting, or relationships, or money and power. This goes beyond a Black president, nonsexist hip-hop, and a zero percent rate of Black-on-Black violence. This is about reclaiming everything that's been taken from us: our culture, our power, and most important our sense of who we are as individuals living in what is supposed to be the most individualistic culture on the planet.

The war is still on, folks, and every generation thus far has done its part. Our great-great-grandparents endured the last of slavery to get us free. Our grandparents got us out of the South. Our parents got us the right to vote and be wherever anyone else was. They made the way for us to be the served instead of the serving, the passengers instead of the driver. And now, what will we make the way for?

I don't sleep the entire night. I lay on my back and see the spirits hovering over my head. I'm restless because they are. I am restless because this isn't the way the story is supposed to end.

She is beautiful, perfection personified. Weighing in at just over nine pounds, she has her father's eyes, ears, and just about his everything else. A day old, her tiny hands give off the fragile scent of new creation. Her eyes, still adjusting, almost always remain closed. She lets out a different sound each time I adjust my arms to cradle her. This is what it's all about.

Olu Babi, a teacher and mentor to me in the Ifa religion, once told me about that perfect feeling of having your child pressed against your chest. I now understand how a baby can change a man, and how the fear of responsibility drives far too many away from the job. I understand that this baby is a gift, but unfortunately not a gift to me.

Assata Ire' Osa Sade Allwood is not my daughter. Instead, she is the child of Konata Kemet and Salathiel Kendrick-Allwood, two of my dearest friends. They got pregnant in the same week we did. But *our* child did not make it to term.

Somewhere after "I'm pregnant" my woman decided that she was having second thoughts, that having a child her first year of law school was something she just couldn't do. She changed her mind again and wanted to keep it a week later when she saw the sonogram. Then a few nights after that she came home drunk and giddy. That next morning she set the appointment for the following Saturday.

It was her choice to make and I stood by her. One swipe of my debit card and she was ready to get it over with. It took five hours for the doctor to arrive and another two before my woman reappeared after the procedure.

I sat there in the waiting area of a clinic with a false name listed on the building's directory. At one point I went out for chips and Twizzlers and encountered a man in his seventies holding a blown-up photo of an aborted fetus. I'd seen dozens of shots like that before but that one stuck with me. He'd made his point, but it was a choice he and his body would never have to make.

I'll always remember the other dudes at the clinic: the Puerto Rican cat with the long hair who confessed he'd been to the place a bunch of times before. There was the tall East Indian guy who looked like he couldn't wait to leave, and the sixteen-year-old white boy who was like a deer in headlights. They had the nerve to be showing cartoons on the tiny TV in the corner. But strangely enough, none of us turned the channel.

We all sat there on those cheap pleather chairs and couches. There was nothing on the wall to admire as the bland fluorescent light beamed down on us. They all had their reasons but I was just there, being supportive, being present, being a dad for just a little while.

Fatherhood is the last thing I ever wanted to start and not finish. It was the one job I thought I could do without fail because I'd had such a good teacher. I could've provided for us all until the end. I could've built the life that would have kept us happy. Yet it was not meant to be. As a matter of fact, she and I are no longer a "we."

Almost a year later she broke down and told me that it was someone else's kid, that she'd sold me a lie because I was the only person she could trust to do what was needed. She had lied for so long because she was too afraid of losing me to trust me with truth. She had lied to herself about the bipolar disorder that had impaired her judgment all the way around. And yet I was the one who was supposed to pick up the pieces. I was supposed to be forgiving and accepting. I was supposed to just go back to being friends again as if the whole affair thing had been nothing but a bad dream. There was probably more intrigue in that than in the rest of this book combined, more facades and snares than one would find in the toughest times Jesse Langley ever had.

I couldn't deal. I swallowed copious amounts of rum and cola. I rolled sticky green into split-open cigars, then lit and inhaled. I collapsed on other people's couches because they felt safer than the home where she'd betrayed me. I avoided her calls and instant messages and put all of our things, including her plastic bracelet from the hospital and the receipt from the clinic, in an album to remember, and closed it, wanting to never see her again. But when I did see her, randomly on a sunny summer afternoon, I saw the guilt wrenching her insides beneath the veneer of prescribed antidepressants, and I understood that blaming her was pointless, that we'd met at a crossroads and then moved down our respective paths. Such is life. Such is love. Such is the end to that part of this tale.

Even from the other side, the Lone Ranger still makes his will known. He entered the dreams of my ex-significant other and told her that she, whom he had never met, was not the woman for me. Many of my father's words about him became spots of dead air on my interview recordings. And just after Christmas 2003, my uncle Tony saw a shadow against the wall in his mother's room and knew it was his father. The youngest son told the spirit to get out of there and it retreated, disappearing right before his eyes.

I began this journey searching for a man I never got to know. What I wanted was a composite sketch of someone I'd seen as both hero and villain, generous father and abusive husband. I thought it would be a matter of Mike Wallacing the right answers out of my family's mouths, about uncovering some secret letter or journal that would instantly make it all clear. I wanted the world to have a record of someone like him, a someone who made the way for greater things for his offspring, someone who bucked the system, got his dream to be real, and still lived to be an old man.

Yet embarking on this tour of Jesse Langley, Sr., has taken me to places I never imagined, up and down the East Coast from suburb to project, and more important into the depths of my own soul.

There are so many pieces to this old man's puzzle. What becomes of the life of a boy who never knows his parents, who is taught to work but never to play? How does he say "I love you" when most likely it was rarely or never said to him? How does he learn to socialize when he's rarely had friends? How does he function in a world full of people better equipped for dealing with one another?

From where I stand, he was not the best husband. I believe he brought clouds to the ray of light he was blessed to have as his life partner. I believe his sons reached adulthood not knowing how to express their emotions to those they cared about. I believe his entire family in one way or another became slaves to his will.

I also know that he gave us joy in just as many ways. Without his work there wouldn't have been a house for a whole neighborhood to grow up in. There wouldn't have been the proper education for a pretty little girl who wanted to become a teacher. There wouldn't have been an ace boon coon for a middle son who needed one, nor a supportive (even if chauvinistic) uncle there in the pews to support a niece during her first trial sermon.

Without him, Jeanette wouldn't be closer to the father she never knew. Lil' Jay wouldn't have had an elder to hear and perceive in his early years. Loretta wouldn't have had a man to replace the one who wasn't around. And I wouldn't have had the need to begin a journey for answers that in the end brought me back to myself.

It's only been in recent years that I've considered the true importance of ancestry, that long ago, the first of those in our bloodlines set out to achieve certain tasks. They could have decided to build a house, or to travel the world, or to create something that would last far beyond the meaning of their little lives. These pledges may not have even been uttered. They could have only been a whisper in the minds of one or two.

But as life and death came for ancestor and elder, as children were born and grew, those whispers somehow stuck, tucked away within the genetic codes of succeeding offspring and quietly affecting the choices of so many individuals to come. As the children of those stolen away, we've become even less aware of what those folk up the line might have experienced, about the legacy and traditions of which we are a part.

Our behavior is shaped by what we see and hear. Our thoughts often become and echo those who we see and hear. Cecil Tyson might have always wanted to write a book. Robert Smith might have always wished to know his grandfather. Thus these things finally filtered down through the generations to me.

It is a great chain of being, a series of links stretching infinitely toward past and future. Searching for my grandfather truly has been searching for myself. Through the eyes and mouths of others I have seen a man with whom I can identify.

I choose solitude over the crowds of my peers and colleagues because we seem to speak different languages. I'm not good at small talk and brownnosing, kicking the scuttlebutt from one place to the other in a crowded room because I don't know how to discuss anything else. I work instead of talking about it. I make things happen instead of announcing them in some huge and grandiose way. My pleasure comes from small, quiet things: watching the summer sun set at the Brooklyn Heights Promenade, cooking quiet dinners for two, enjoying films without the commentary of the chicken heads talking in seats behind me because everyone they know does the same thing.

I can also be angry when I don't know how to express things. I can explode when best-laid plans fail miserably. I am painfully loyal to families of both blood and spirit. And I better not have daughters because I'll expect a lot from any boy who crosses my threshold.

I never would've seen these things if I hadn't decided to look, if the man in the room upstairs hadn't moved on. He'd still be that taciturn old guy with the not so stylish clothes and an affinity for all kinds of pork. He would've still been a stranger I assumed to be out of reach. He would've always remained a Lone Ranger.

My father smiled when I told him that that was what Jesse had chosen to call himself. Pop didn't think it was true; it was only the perception of someone who'd always felt isolated even when he had so many around him who set their watches by his every move. But the truth doesn't matter if it's not what you feel. The world being round doesn't mean a thing if you don't believe it.

My grandfather is with me now as I bang my fingertips against this worn keyboard. He speaks in this narrative despite his reticence. He and I are part of the same great chain, one that will never be broken, no matter how often time, evil, and circumstance attempt it. We are both men following a path cleared for us long ago, warriors pushing toward a victory only truly understood by those in another realm.

"He always respected what you chose to do," my mother informed me after one of our interview sessions. "He was a guy who worked for himself, who made his own money, and he saw that in you."

Had it been my house I might have chosen the porch at 1341 Childress. Had it been my life I would have chosen Sally Helen the moment I saw her. Yet at nearly a third his age I'd seen things he never thought of. I've traveled out of the country and have been on television time and time again. My words have become available for anyone to read, and I always have a new story for the family while most of theirs generally remain the same. You could say I've kept our chain moving forward. I've become the beneficiary of his wisdom, sins, successes, failures, loves, hates, habits, pet peeves, and fascinations. But they are no more mine than they were his, merely elements being passed down a never-ending line, elements I too will offer up to the next link when it's my time to move on.